NO OTHER PLACE

An Anthology of Poetry from
Aberdeen University Review
1913–1995

Edited by Ian A Olson

with an Introduction by
George Bruce

TUCKWELL PRESS

First published in Great Britain in 1995 by
Tuckwell Press Ltd
The Mill House
Phantassie
East Linton
East Lothian
EH40 3DG
Scotland

ISBN 1 898410 63 1

Cataloguing-in-Publication Data:
A catalogue record for this book is available
on request from the British Library

Typeset by Hewer Text Composition Services, Edinburgh
Printed by Athenaeum Press Ltd

To Theodore and Harold Watt

CONTENTS

Editor's Note			x
Introduction, by George Bruce			xiv
Alexander, Kenneth	*On Climbing Beinn Hiant*	1992	1
Angus, William	*The Chaplains' Court*	1971	2
Baird, Edward	*The Deid Cat*	1954	3
Bell, Harry	*The Jilted Queyn*	1972	4
Bottomley, Gordon	*On the New Memorial*	1931	5
Brown, A J Y	*The Exile*	1942	6
Brown, George Mackay	*To Sister Margaret*	1993	7
Bruce, George	*To a Buchan Fisherman*	1941	8
	Snowdrops in March	1943	9
Buchan, David	*Curtain Up*	1960	10
Caie, J M	*Kirsty and the Gravedigger*	1929	11
	The Road	1931	12
Cairns, David	*I know that soon my journey will be done*	1990	13
	Song	1989	13
	Scotland in Early Summer	1990	13
Calder, W M	*Laudatio Funebris – Old Style*	1921	14
Carnegie, Agnes C	*Todeserfahrung* (from Rilke)	1949	15
Christie, William	*An Unco Hairst*	1956	16
	From Sappho	1963	16
Clark, Ivo M	*Atween the Gloamin' an the Mirk*	1950	17
Cook, John	*The Smith*	1931	21
Craigmyle, Elizabeth	*On the Evening of a Funeral*	1920	22

Daiches, David	*Balconies*	1992	23
Dawson, Elizabeth T	*The Micht-Hae-Been*	1953	24
Diack, Hunter	*The White Spaces*	1989	25
	The Signpost	1991	28
Dow, Alexander R	*Provost Davidson and the Heroes of Harlaw*	1977	30
Draper, Ronald	*Memorial*	1992	33
Elwolde, John	*Death in the West*	1986	34
Farquhar, Alice M M	*April Day*	1949	35
Ferguson, A S	*Casida of the Branches (after Lorca)*	1939	36
Fraser, Olive	*The Dipper's Nest*	1976	37
	The King's Student	1946	37
Garden, R J B	*The Lost Wine (after Paul Valéry)*	1994	38
Garry, Flora	*The Cat*	1952	39
	Sutherland Street, W.2	1951	40
	Bog Cotton	1959	42
Geddes, Arthur	*The Brig o' Balgownie*	1948	44
Gordon, Donald	*Strange Music*	1939	45
	Sang for a Lost Lover	1983	46
Gourlay, David	*Auld Jeames*	1956	47
Graham, Cuthbert	*For Dr Nan Shepherd*	1979	48
Gray, Alexander	*In a Music Hall*	1928	49
Gray, John	*A Paraphrase*	1954	50
Greig, Gavin	*Song*	1995	51
Grierson, H J C	*Love's Hour*	1925	52
Hardy, Thomas	*The Youth Who Carried a Light*	1916	53
	Aberdeen (April 1905)	1928	53

Harries, Harry R	*Echoes at King's*	1979	54
Harrower, J	*From the Greek Anthology*	1922	55
Harvey, G Rowntree	*The Dream and the Deed* (extract)	1931	56
	Bennachie	1926	56
Henderson, Dorothy E	*Bus Journey Home*	1977	57
Henderson, Hamish	*Lament for the Son* (after Govoni)	1987	58
Hughson, Irene	*Daffodils*	1967	60
Jenkins, May C	*The Exile*	1960	61
	Roads in Rain	1967	61
Kidd, D A	*To Postumus*	1946	62
Kynoch, Douglas	*Nine Gweed Rizzens*	1983	63
	A Young Chiel (after Chénier)	1986	64
Lawrence, W Gordon	*Middle Age Love* (after Tagore)	1986	65
	Exiles	1979	65
Logan, John B	*Wee Johnnie Frost*	1925	66
	Glory Departed	1975	67
Lothian, J M	*I will walk proudly on St Andrew's Day*	1951	68
Lumsden, M S	*The Chackie-Mull i the Wud*	1959	69
Macdonald, Alastair	*Vaux-Le-Vicomte*	1986	70
Mackenzie, A C	*Contra Mundum*	1940	71
Mackenzie, Agnes Mure	*Artemisia*	1925	72
	Silvius to Phoebe	1926	72
McLaren, Colin A	*Documents 1746–1790*	1977	73
MacLeod, Anne	*Icarus*	1990	75
	Oran Mor	1990	75

Mearns, Isobel M	*Orchestra*	1939	76
Milne, Royston J	*The Steen Sodger*	1958	78
Miner, Virginia Scott	*Roots*	1975	79
Mitchell, J Leslie (Lewis Grassic Gibbon)	*To Marguerite ('Peggy')*	1989	80
Montgomery, Mary	*Cha Mhòr (Almost)*	1993	82
Morrice, Ken	*Buchan*	1961	83
	Nigg	1962	84
	Domiciliary Visit	1992	85
Munro, Robin	*Patterns*	1975	86
	Sonata	1974	86
Murray, Charles	*'Aiberdeen Awa' '*	1913	87
	Horace I. 9.	1914	88
	Fate Furls the Totum	1927	89
Oelsner, Geoffrey A	*Song For Aberdeen*	1971	90
Olson, Ian A	*Strathconon*	1985	93
Philsooph, H	*A Mirage is not a Mirage*	1989	94
Raitt, Douglas S	*The Blessin' o' Learnin'*	1945	95
Rinker, Linda Jean	*For Anne*	1965	96
	Sonnet for September	1967	96
Ritchie, Christine M	*Dementia*	1991	97
	Myaav	1991	97
Robertson, Edith Anne	*The Artificial*	1959	98
Robertson, Robin	*Dunnottar Castle*	1980	99
Rorie, David	*The Deil and Jock MacNeil*	1925	100
Rush, Christopher	*If only you would fall again into my heart*	1994	107
	Lines for Patricia	1994	108
Sadler, Glenn Edward	*Academic Regret*	1966	109

Scott, Alexander M	*Snow*	1946	110
Simpson, John Watt	*'Ilium'*	1916	114
Sinton, Thomas	*Heraclitus*	1920	115
Smith, George Adam	*Old Aberdeen, October, 1915*	1935	116
Smith, Harry	*'The Thing that's Deen'*	1922	117
Smith, Iain Crichton	*Only The Sea Remains*	1948	118
	Return to Aberdeen University	1987	119
Stuart, Alan D	*Memories*	1988	121
	Seagulls	1988	121
	A Shirt Box Tied With Twine	1991	122
Symon, Mary	*The Glen's Muster Roll*	1915	124
Taylor, Rachel Annand	*Ballad Song of West and East*	1944	126
Thomson, A L	*Lament for a Highlander*	1977	129
Thomson, Derick	*Fever*	1963	130
	Smuaintean Ann An Cafe An Glaschu (*Thoughts in a Glasgow Café*)	1987	132
Tucker, A Christopher	*Uway Tay Eiburdeen*	1977	133
Walker, Thea	*Happy Nostalgia*	1977	134
Watson, Roderick	*Winterclimb*	1973	135
Watson, William	*To Aberdeen*	1935	136
Wavell, Lord	*A Ballade of Bereavement*	1948	137
Wood, Kenneth	*In Memoriam Edwin Muir*	1964	138
	The Brochs of Glenelg	1967	139
Yuill, W E	*The Roman Fountain* (after Meyer)	1962	140

EDITOR'S NOTE

Some twelve years ago I was asked by Eric Morrison, the previous editor of the *Aberdeen University Review*, to contribute an overview entitled 'Seventy-Five Years of the *Review*'. I was so struck then by the range and quality of the poetry I found (and the fact of its subsequent appearance in numerous collections) that I determined one day to publish an anthology. Thanks to the generosity of the Aberdeen University Alumnus Association – which publishes the *Review* – this book now appears, to celebrate the Quincentenary of the University.

In making my initial selection I copied all the poems within fifty-five volumes from 1913 to 1995. As I did so I noticed that they fell naturally into some four categories (although with many overlaps); these groupings in their turn reflected the characteristics of the University, of its history and geography, and of its graduates.

Aberdeen University, founded in 1495 by Papal Bull almost as a last act of faith before the storm of the Reformation engulfed the Christian world, has always existed within two worlds. Her founder, the good Bishop Elphinstone, gained both his Foundation Bull from the Pope (the otherwise notorious Borgia) and support from the generous and cultured James IV who was to throw his life away impetuously at Flodden, by emphasising the pressing needs of the region – which included the Highlands and Islands. The 'precious pearl of knowledge' was vital in order to create graduates who would serve this region and the Kingdom in every possible way, devoting their lives to its welfare and common good. But to achieve this, the University had to be part of an international world of knowledge and learning; it was therefore specifically established in the likeness of the great universities of Paris and Bologna, and started as it meant to go on by recruiting its first Principal from Paris.

Five hundred years later, it was gratifying to see that the poetry from its journal still reflected the University's two worlds, the regional and the international. The general groupings I found could loosely be described as (a) local/regional celebratory, (b) work in Scots, especially the vigorous North-east 'Doric', (c) writings in English, and (d) translations, mainly of European writers. Although the contribution in Gaelic was relatively small, the quality was high, from Thomas Sinton to Derick Thomson (and I have attempted since becoming Editor in 1987 to encourage contributions in this language).

Although, as might be expected, the quality of the local/regional poetry might vary, the intensity of feeling expressed by both native and adopted Aberdonians remained constant. This is reflected in my choice of title, taken from the Bishop Elphinstone speech in G. Rowntree Harvey's *The Dream and the Deed* (1931) which starts, 'I love this place, all seasons of the year', and includes

> No other place
> I've seen sees autumn come with richer gold,
> With lovelier tapestries at dawn or set
> Of sun.

(I should add at this point that it seemed important, especially when selecting from this category, not to let present-day taste predominate completely, for nostalgia, even when sentimental, is a potent force, and can still appeal to even the most hardened.)

As might be expected, there was much good poetry in Scots, for had not Charles Murray himself supported the early issues with his contributions? He was to be followed by many others whose work reflected the thriving living language that the University's hinterland supports to this day – no need for dictionary Lallans. Many contributors, though, have chosen to write in English (often as an addition to their work in Scots or Gaelic) and many achieved fame and recognition in this medium, building upon their liberal university education. (This was not always an unmitigated blessing; when I asked Flora Garry why she had tightened and transformed *Bog Cotton* (1959) for publication in her collected poems, she replied, 'To make it better, of course! Too Eng. Lit!')

Aberdeen's international, especially European, perspective is clearly reflected in the considerable body of translation in the *Review*, the Greek and Latin in the early days giving way to renderings of such as Valéry, Rilke and Lorca. English was not always employed, for Scots and even Gaelic were popular. (Sad to say, I have excluded the often beautiful translations *into* Latin or Greek that appeared in early issues, judging, perhaps wrongly, that too few nowadays would understand or appreciate them.)

Although I hope readers will be as impressed as I was by the poets who have appeared in the *Review* – George Mackay Brown, George Bruce, J M Caie, David Daiches, Olive Fraser, Flora Garry, Alexander Gray, Thomas Hardy, Douglas Kynoch, Agnes Mackenzie, Anne MacLeod, Ken Morrice, Leslie Mitchell, Robin Munro, David Rorie, Christopher Rush, Alexander Scott, Thomas Sinton, Iain Crichton Smith, Mary Symon, Rachel Annand Taylor, Derick Thomson, to name but a few – they may be surprised to find that some poets are unexpectedly missing – graduates such as J C Milne, Nan Shepherd or Alistair Mackie. Perhaps they sought a wider audience for their work (although the *Review* in fact circulates worldwide and appears on the shelves of libraries from Moscow to Montreal); some were invited to write for other journals and some, indeed, may have been unaware of the *Review*'s interest in publishing poetry. It is also clear that *Alma Mater*, the student magazine published from 1883 to 1965, attracted the writings of many – Rachel Annand Taylor, Agnes 'Mure' Mackenzie, Nan Shepherd and David Rorie. I did consider combining selections from *Alma Mater* with the *Review* poetry, but an excellent *Alma Mater* anthology was published in its heyday in 1919, and, furthermore, throughout most of its life few of the poems it published were signed.

'Outside' writers have often featured in the *Review*, beginning with a grateful Thomas Hardy (Aberdeen was the first university to recognise his worth with an honorary degree in 1905), and culminating in more recent offerings from established writers such as David Daiches and George Mackay Brown. In some ways this is not surprising, for the *Review* was not only the first general postgraduate journal to be published but also appears to be the last in existence in Britain. Over the years its contents have been harvested for numerous anthologies, for it has been a major publisher of poetry throughout its existence. A glance at the contents page of this anthology will demonstrate also that many of its 'own' poets have achieved wider recognition and even fame; many, however, have been content to publish only the occasional poem for their fellow graduates.

In making this compilation I was most grateful for the help of the members of the Alumnus Association, especially Dina Garden, Marjorie Leith, Sandy Mackenzie and Alison Milne and for the generous assistance of Donald Meek and the staff of the University and City District Libraries. Every effort was made to contact the poets or their families; all authors I was able to identify agreed without hesitation to donate their work. I am especially grateful to the families of those no longer with us and should like to thank Nan Argo (Gavin Greig), Elsie Diack, Molly Gordon, Rhea Martin (J Leslie Mitchell) and Catherine Scott, together with the David Rorie Society and Canongate Press (Olive Fraser) for their kind permissions.

The only (mild) argument I have had with contributors was with those who would have preferred me to publish revised versions of their poems. All eventually agreed with my principle of publishing the originals (typographical errors apart). This gives an accurate and unvarnished portrait of the contents of the *Review*. Furthermore it shows the development of many established poets whose early work appeared in its pages; I hope literary scholars will find this of interest. My main regret is having to set aside so many poems – almost four hundred – for reasons of space.

George Bruce has generously capped many years of encouragement and support to me by providing an Introduction in which he stands back sufficiently from the University he loves to cast a kindly but critical eye over the contents of this anthology. Although I have attempted to be even-handed, my selection is, however, entirely personal, coloured by love for the strengths of the *Review* and of the *universitas* which supports it – a consistency which has assimilated change, a universality based on a deep sense of place, a modernity rooted in an ancient yet living tradition, and a feeling for the warmth of time. In her last book of poetry Rachel Annand Taylor expressed it better:

> Oh! that's a city to be born in.
>   The pure air kindles you, and witty
> Your mind goes dancing. To learn scorn in,
>   Oh! that's a city.
>
> The sea-birds cry wild things above, in
>   The tender and the stainless sky.
> Oh! that's a city to learn love in,
>   Where sea-birds cry.
>
> Under the Crown that dreams of Flodden
>   And Borgia in scarlet gown
> Youth lightly treads where Youth has trodden
>   Under the Crown.
>
> In Aberdeen, through years of splendour,
>   You may ride mailed in gold and green.
> Ironic folk to Youth are tender
>   In Aberdeen.

Readers who have difficulty with Scots words in any of the poems that follow might care to consult *The Concise Scots Dictionary* (1985), Editor-in-chief Mairi Robinson.

INTRODUCTION

by George Bruce

I n his Foreword to the first number of the *Aberdeen University Review*, Sir George Adam Smith, the Principal of Aberdeen University, wrote:

> The contents will comprise summary records of the Proceedings of the Court, the Senatus and the Council, with notices of all educational and administrative changes, as well as of new grants, gifts and bequests; detailed accounts of the various departments and curricula, with reports of special studies and researches, abstracts of notable papers and lectures, studies in the history of the University, biographies and bibliographies, occasional reports from other Universities, correspondence on University questions, and articles on letters, philosophy, science and education.

Such weighty and necessary content – 'these contents are proper to every University Review' (the Principal) – gives no prospect for including that which exists to please by being itself, poetry. Yet poetry was not outwith the directive, for the Foreword continues:

> We shall endeavour besides to inspire our own with the memories, the atmosphere and the genius which are peculiar to Aberdeen. Her founders planned her on more liberal lines than any other Scottish school of the time . . . delayed for centuries by scantiness of resources, she found a moral compensation for this in the close touch which she has always maintained with the popular life about her. . . . We shall be happy, if, in addition to the record of such facts and opinions, we are able to reinforce through the *Review* – whether by prose or verse – those impulses, immeasurable by statistics and independent of curricula and degrees, by which the atmosphere and associations of our University have moulded the character of her students.

Brave words! But chance and circumstance might well play too great a part to allow their full implementation over the years. *Alma Mater* and later *Gaudie* were natural outlets for the expression in verse of student wit and sentiment, but thereafter the committed practitioner would look for a readership primarily interested in poetry, and one not restricted to the alumni of a single university. Yet the fact is that poetry has been available, and has been featured, throughout eighty years of publication, and beyond. The contributors have been, and are, established poets, aspiring poets, occasional versifiers, academics venturing, generally through translation – one thinks of Professor Harrower and Professor Grierson – honorary graduates, including a general, the Chancellor Earl Wavell, and the renowned novelist and poet, Thomas Hardy, and also some who have no academic connection with the university. How has this come about? The first motivation, surely, is affection for the *Alma Mater*, but the credit for directing this affection and sense of loyalty is due to the Editors, who in varying degrees saw this contribution as worthy. However, one's expectation of the contents of this anthology must differ from the norm where the Editor has the right to select from what he regards as the 'best' of a poet's work. Here he will find himself with the promising work of the young poet before he or she has found an individual style, though this makes the case a special interest. There are names missing from this selection which one might have expected to see, such as Alistair Mackie, the Doric poet John C Milne, the Gaelic poets Donald Macaulay and John Munro, and, though not essentially poets, Eric Linklater and Nan Shepherd. This is the chance factor at work, for, sadly, they never submitted their work to the *Review*. On the other side, thanks to the imagination of the present Editor, there are the unexpected bonuses culminating in such writers as Mary Montgomery and David Daiches, both in Gaelic and English convincing voices. All these diverse talents, characters, professions make this publication a unique occasion.

As if in response to the Principal's reference to 'the atmosphere and the genius which are peculiar to Aberdeen', there are two poems on the city in the first number of the magazine – October 1913. The first, *To Aberdeen* by William Watson, begins strongly:

> At the great dance and upleap of the year
> I came.

It continues in a grand poetic style:

> O city of the pallid brow austere.
> Grey, wintry-featured, sea-throned Aberdeen!

Here is the poet-visitor paying tribute in such resounding vocables, that we may be more conscious of their effect than of the place itself. The poem differs markedly from *Aiberdeen Awa* by the exile Charles Murray, which, while modest in intention, has the stir of 'popular life' – to which the Principal referred – in such lines as:

> I fain would dook in Dee aince mair
> An' clatter doon the market stair –
> O the caller dulse an' partans there!
> The fish-wives mutches braw!

There was not room enough to develop such active imagery in the poem for it was a toast 'to the Aberdeen University Club of South Africa', but it takes only a few words to reveal the vitality and assurance of the Aberdeenshire tongue.

The visitor seeks out 'the atmosphere and the genius', as did Thomas Hardy in *Aberdeen* (1905), published originally in *Alma Mater*, to which he refers as 'too grey and cold', but in the last phrase in the poem he discovers that here there was 'the stability of the time'. The poem Hardy later contributed to the *Review*, *The Youth who carried a Light* (1916), is also a quest for an inner meaning. He clearly glimpsed the enormous, and continuous, strength of Aberdeenshire community life (even with its near-impenetrable speech to the visitor) in his *Aberdeen (April 1905)*.

The subjects and interests of the poems in the *Review* range far beyond Aberdeen, but this focus reveals the wide range of styles accepted on this subject alone by the several Editors, running from the rather aureate song of Rachel Annand Taylor to the vernacular. The first number witnessed the polarities, though it is evident that the Editor valued the native speech from the publication of poems by Charles Murray in the first three numbers. That sense that 'the reality, which is the root of all poetry', according to J M Synge, may be immediately experienced in poems in the Doric, does not mean it is excluded from poems in English, of which there are many written about the city and the University with deep affection. Not that affection guarantees success, but those, I suggest, which key their note to the subject, and keep near the nerve of common speech, have the greater chance of lasting. Take Geoffrey Oelsner's *Song for Aberdeen* (1971), for instance, which embraces all aspects of the city:

> There were sounds of people
> singing, fighting,
> pivoting from pain to sleep
> to morning hope.
> The woman in the shop
> selling pastries.

All taken 'into the roar of the sea' and so given a context in the 'stability of the time':

> So it has been
> since before Elphinstone,
> before St Machar's,
> before even the oldest rainbeaten gravemarkers.
> Since the first settlers
> laid stone upon stone,
> spoke together in a tongue
> closer to the wind's syntax
> than our own.

No atmospherics. Experience of consequence to the writer, and to his people, is presented and scrutinised. This the true poet sees as a responsibility, as in Ken Morrice's *Nigg* (1962), in which the poet contemplates writing an epitaph for his fishermen ancestors:

> Time alone separates the dull red
> Granite of these cliffs and the red
> Clay in the kirkyard yonder.
> As I stand on this gray day,
> With scarce a breath to sunder

xvi

> The wetness of air and sea,
> Let my living and my dead
> Surround me. Let them say
> Who carried the sea upon his back,
> What fish sucked the marrow from whose bones.

Such proper admiration, but Ken Morrice takes the argument a step
further:

> I would have written an epitaph
> . . . .
> But the whistling peewit mocks my mood
> And anyway they would not have understood.

Recognition, understanding and acceptance of what must be accepted,
and this is what Iain Crichton Smith asks for in his *Return to Aberdeen
University* (1987). Having noted the changes in Aberdeen – 'the cinemas
are gone,/replaced by Bingo' – he focuses on King's:

> We have lived since then through the most violent times,
>
> but the quadrangles remain quiet as once before.
> I push (extraordinarily) this well-known door.
> I am an explorer but what I explore
>
> is the past not present.

He is discovering the self that was and he comments:

> how can I face the idealist I knew . . .?

He answers his query about the two selves:

> So let us walk together down this street,
> a father and a son perhaps, in light
> of supernatural clarity and granite
>
> sparkling with a memory and a present fire.
> The cobblestones are shaky. O for fear
> that we fail or falter let us walk together
>
> in the common merciful air so bright and green
> in ancient solid vanishing Aberdeen.

The complex of the inner and outer experience – the solidity of the
place as witnessed in time past, the fragility of the varying self –
projected through the poem is a rare achievement of honesty, but it
could not have been achieved without the availability of a style distilled
from the currency of common speech. As one goes through the eighty
years of Scottish poetry I am aware of the style being increasingly

available. Iain Crichton Smith has the advantage of working in two traditions, Gaelic and English, and this development, even from the few examples in the *Review*, may be seen in the Gaelic poems of Mary Montgomery (1993) and Derick Thomson (1987).

This staple of verse, it seems to me, has provided a way of talking in poetry which has allowed poems of character and merit to be made by sometimes very occasional practitioners in the art – the Chancellor, Sir Kenneth Alexander, himself, in his *On Climbing Beinn Hiant* (1992); Professor David Daiches, though with an international reputation as scholar-critic, with his firm, yet poignant, *Balconies* (1992); and the current Editor of the *Review*, Ian A Olson, though in his case, it is hard to believe that the clarity, firmness and subtle ironies of *Strathconon* (1985) have been achieved without a deal of previous writing. How far a 'poetry of facts' (MacDiarmid) can be taken successfully is witnessed in Colin A McLaren's *Documents 1746–1790* (1977). Ultimately the reach is beyond the proposition. It may merely begin there. Take, for instance, Hunter Diack's *The White Spaces* (1989) – a vigorous and probing mind runs throughout. In the end there is song, and when the writer feels it is made 'one step from extinction', there is no doubting its truth, nor intensity. I refer to Anne MacLeod's *Oran Mor* (1990).

This said, and put behind, so that simply the poem be allowed to talk to us, there are excitements and moving utterances in this book that proceed from urgencies of need to set down what must be set down, though not possible without craftmanship. There is the splendid and painful *Lament for the Son* (1987) by Hamish Henderson, a translation from a long poem by Corrado Govani; and there are other translations which become poems in their own right, amongst them *Cassida of the Branches* (1939) from the Spanish of Lorca, by A S Ferguson: no translation, as might have been expected had space allowed, from the erstwhile Professor of Political Economy, Sir Alexander Gray. His contribution, in English, *In a Music Hall* (1928), is a curiously touching vision of the evanescence of youth as he sees a young girl on stage. He had already published translations of Heine in Scots in 1920, which mode was to give him his reputation as poet. Frequently, if not generally, the contributions to the *Review* by graduates came from their pens before their particular style, or even language, had been determined, but Rory Watson's *Family Group* (1969) registers a style which seems to spring from the subject itself, which he was to develop. Alexander Scott, on the other hand, whose reputation rests securely on his poems in Scots, contributes poems in English, but with such verve in them as to be a prelude to his later depiction of Aberdeen, *Heart of Stone*, a poem not entirely complimentary to the city.

Throughout the eighty years of verse drawn from the *Review* there is heard the traditional voice of the community of the North-East. The 'Doric' is a tongue which can give the fact and the sensation of the fact immediately, as in:

> Fyles the cankle o' a kirk-bell, fyles the vrattle o' a cairt
> Or a wheeshin whirrication faur the pertick echt her nest.
>> *The Steen Sodger* – Royston J Milne (1958)

Admittedly, Roy Milne has exploited 'whirr' but the flexibility of the language allows for this. For translation it is admirable, as in Charles Murray's 'Horace I. 9' (1914):

> Drift oxter deep haps Benachie,
> Aneth its birn graens ilka tree . . .

Compared with Allan Ramsay's

> Look up to Pentland's towring taps,
> Buried beneath great wreaths of snaw

it seems to me Benachie is a fairer exchange for Soracte than 'Pentlands Tap':

> . . . But still an' on I'll see,
> In my min's benmost nyeuk, I'll sweir,
> Like bleezin cwyles o' caul' green fire,
> Your twa een glowering straacht at me.
> *The Cat*, Flora Garry (1952)
> from Baudelaire's *Les Fleurs du Mal*

Such intensities provided by the Scots, and also such doon-taakin fun when the classical muses encounter the Doric:

> Melpomene was mumpin;
> And her een were rubbit reid;
> . . . .
> Thalia, she was scraichin
> Like a half-dementit hen.
> *Nine Gweed Rizzens* (Kynoch 1983)

At these levels the use of the tongue cannot be surpassed. It has an irrepressible spirit, never more attractive than when invoking the absurd. Its rootedness lets it deal with the products of 'high' cultures with confident ease. Too much confidence, however, may have been placed in the evocation of sentiment, which may give a poem a comfortable conclusion, but at the expense of the doubting and seeking mind. Edward Baird's *The Deid Cat* (1954), however, has that temper about it from its opening lines, which promises it is to be a poem of character. It begins:

> Fin I wis bit fower
> I kilt the wee cat.

The poem makes it clear the killing was not out of malice but because the child thought if he 'flacht it sair' the cat would play with him. The poem ends:

> Ma mither raged and syne she grat,
> Mair for her loon than for her cat.

No yielding to the stock pathetic response but concern for the child's humanity in the future.

The remarkable fact is that by 1983, as Ian Olson then stated, 'The *Review* has published over four hundred poems by some two hundred poets.' The designation is optimistic, and while numbers cannot vouch for quality, they point to the word given by the Principal in 1913 – liberal. This liberality has taken a greater significance as the *Review*, in the late eighties and nineties, as well as publishing a poetry showing the diverse colours of Scotland, from George Mackay Brown south, has become, through the commissioning and publication of articles, a participant in contemporary literary discussions. Through this anthology one can now see this generous policy of the present Editor as the flourish on a tree planted over eighty years ago.

By Kenneth Alexander

ON CLIMBING BEINN HIANT

There is something holy about these rocks,
Celestial, transcendent, immanent and serene.
They may serve a purpose,
But it is far from clear.

Fifty-eight million years ago
There were many convulsions,
Omnipotent, supernatural, unmeasurable.
Then two million years later
God's sense of the appropriate
Moved the earth again
To put the Blessed Mountain up a bit,
And MacLean's Nose out of joint.

Has He waited fifty-six million years
For us to discover His purpose?

Perhaps we have all been too busy
Worrying about the meaning of life?
A fairly obvious thing, surely,
Compared to assessing the virtue
Of all these cryptic stones.

(1992)

By William Angus

THE CHAPLAINS' COURT

This house has been a house of prayer
Where men who served God's table dwelt,
And this has been a house of fear
Where ill was done and evil felt.

Maybe it's been a house of care
Where menseful folk have pinched and saved;
No doubt it's been a house of cheer
Where toasts were pledged and trysts were made.

Now let the house with joy be filled
That bairns may grow in strength and grace,
While you and I move on towards eld
With cheerful, douce and even pace.

(1971)

By Edward Baird

THE DEID CAT

Fan I wis bit fower
I killt the wee cat;
And muckle shame's been mine for that.
Nae luck I've had in a' my life,
Neither siller nor a wife.

In it cam' fae the caul byre
Tae dry itsel' afore the fire;
It widna play, it widna eat,
But purred an' licket at its feet.

I took a stick and flacht it sair;
I thocht it wis the richt remeid.
I lacht tae see it streekit there,
Until I learnt that it wis deid.

Ma mither raged and syne she grat,
Mair for her loon than for her cat.

(1954)

3

By Harry Bell

THE JILTED QUEYN

Abeen, the stars are shinan clear,
Ootbye, a cock begins tae crow,
Noo canny doun the kitchen stairs
An rake the embers till they glow.

O bonnie, bonnie is the bleeze
As up the lum the wee sparks fly,
Quaet-like I watch the flame,
Then aa at aince I start to sigh.

For suddenly I fell a stoun,
Richt through ma hairt it gangs fu' sair,
Oh Jamie in ma thochts ye smiled
But ye'll come back tae me nae mair.

The blindan tear is in ma ee,
A broken hairt's nae easy mendit;
But I maun start ma lang day's darg
Oh God, gin it were speedy endit.

(1972)

By Gordon Bottomley

ON THE NEW MEMORIAL TO BISHOP ELPHINSTONE IN THE CHAPEL OF HIS FOUNDATION OF KING'S COLLEGE AT ABERDEEN

What a great pattern of vicissitude
This figure, cast for everlasting, is:
It stands for something lost through centuries –
Another figure, shattered as soon as hewed:
Wise British hands have shaped it, yet indued
Its heart with this bronze flesh in Venice's
Fostering; and the Adriatic seas
Took it to their deep care when war ensued.

What a great pattern of steadfastness is here?
A father at last among his sons is sleeping
Visibly, here returning to where most dear
Young names are lately graven, their great Term keeping –
His sons who here with him are honoured apart
For deeds that could have healed his broken heart.

(1931)

By A J Y Brown

THE EXILE

The oleanders flower more slowly,
And the angel fishes play;
I remember; green the island,
White the terrace, blue the bay.

The pigeon-berries fall in autumn
And now must do, thro' the sun,
Falling, now, to cover over
Last year's leaves, and days undone.

Another year, another summer.
Look, the blue-birds, they will say.
Sparkle the sun; breeze, bend the grasses:
This is next year, now, they say.

(1942)

By George Mackay Brown

TO SISTER MARGARET AT SACRED HEART CONVENT ON ST MAGNUS DAY 1992

Outside my window, daffodils
Dance in the north wind.
In another garden
A blackbird
Clothes, before leaves, a tree in song.

It is Saint Magnus Day.

But for that company of heroes
But for those
Whose blood purified the roots and sources
The daffodills
Would be a measurable disturbance of earth and air today,
That blackbird
A graph on a cold grid of sound.

But the poor still dance (thank God.)
Because of the saints
We, a throng out of winter
Dance now in coats brighter than Solomon.

(1993)

By George Bruce

TO A BUCHAN FISHERMAN

SEA TALK

Night holds the past, the present is manifest in day,
In day activity, but night shuts the door –
And within the mind hints of your old powers,
Recollections of your associate, the sea.

Now, this night, in tribute I write you
And have you, your boys, your wife, in mind
The better for not being there where you are.
Too much business there with winch running,
Pulleys slipping, hawsers, horses, men, lorries, herring;
Besides, being a cranner, I must note the fish
And see to the salt. But here
I remember again your boys on the beach at sundown,
Their graips at sods of sand,
Their hands' flash for bait,
Behind – sandhills with grass,
In front the sea, that sea that binds to it
The cottage on the cliff-top or on the shore,
Invades the ears of the boy, enters his eyes, binds him
And the crustacea – monsters of the sea pools.

Consider the spider crab.
From the rock, half-rock itself, pin-head eyes project;
The mechanism of movement awkward, legs propelled,
A settlement for paradise, for limpet;
Passionless stone in the world of motion.
The pounded shells, a broken razor,
Mussel, fan, speak as much life.

O dark-haired fisherman who know the tides
And proper prices for the catch,
Here is the image of your skull.
Who will tell upon the shingle beach
Which the shell splinter, which the particle of the skull,
Long bleached by the flow and ebb?

The sea binds the village,
Its salt constricts the pasture behind,
Its gale fastens the bent grass before,
Its fog is in the nostrils of the boy.
Your iron ship, a novelty to sea's age,
Puts out. Sea gives tongue to greater
Fears, deeds, terrors, than you can tell.
It's articulate in the crab, the hermit, spider, partan;

8

These tell the knowledge in your bone.
Over these your boat slips
And down to these grope line and nets.

Here breed the initiates of life
In rock-chambers and on the floor beneath tide,
Beneath sway and trouble, undisturbed.

(1941)

SNOWDROPS IN MARCH

Curious that these long-overdue February flowers
Should come almost unexpected to our
Remote world: and they suspensive in cold and light
Now remain even in their proper powers.

Like a legend, dreamt of, not hoped on,
Nor for us, these, delicate, of perfect leaf
And petal, but secret hold
For other Springs their promissory note.

(1943)

By David Buchan

CURTAIN UP

'Clear the stage now please.'
The wardrobe mistress fixes
The final safety pin
And flutters off.
The cast whisper throaty
'Good Lucks'
The producer mutters
'God help you'
And disappears to the bar.
'Thirty seconds now please.'
A trembling silence descends.
'For God's sake shut
That dressing-room door.'
The stage manager raises his arm,
The swift check-over glance,
'O.K.? – Right!'
He vanishes into the wings
The button is pressed
The curtains hiss open
The footlights glare up
Beyond, a glassy sea of faces
Awaiting the world you
Are about to create.

(1960)

By J M Caie

KIRSTY AND THE GRAVEDIGGER

Ay, Kirsty, ye besom, ye're quait kin' noo,
That's mair nor ye eesed tae be, sober or fou;
See, here's a gweed spaadfu', I'll tramp it weel in –
It's the first time I've managed tae sattle yer din.

I saw by the name-plate it's seventy year
Ye've keepit the place in a bonny-like steer,
An' noo, though I'm tell't he's a coorse kin' o' chiel,
I'se warran' ye're mair nor a match for the deil.

I'll birze ye weel doon, ye mischievious jaud,
For in life ye were neither tae bin' nor tae haud,
An' still, though, ye're deid an' ye're singin' gey sma',
Though ye're streekit an' kistit an' beeriet an' a',

Ye limmer, ye'd like, gin ye'd only the poo'r
Tae come claverin' up throu' the mools and the stoor,
But, dod, I'll mak siccar an' hap ye up ticht
Neth the aul' muckle stane or I bid ye gweed-nicht.

It winna be mowse winnin' oot o' this grave
Gin ye seek, fin the time comes, tae rise wi' the lave,
But, mebbe, fin Gaabriel's trumpet'll soun',
They'll howk oot the boddom an' lat ye gyang doon.

(1929)

11

THE ROAD

Doon the close an' up the loanin',
   An' syne the big road, braid an' free,
Tae lead ye hine ow'r the hills far the sooth win' sings
An' a gowden mist i' the mornin' sunlicht clings,
   Or awa' til a dreamlan' sea.

Doon the close an' up the loanin',
   Its aye the road was the gait for me;
An' files I set my he'rt tae the lang stey brae,
An' files, fan the hills were dark an' the mist was gray,
   I socht for my dreamlan' sea.

Baith licht o' fit n' sair forfochen
   I trod the big road, hard an' lang.
But ne'er could reach the sea, far my dreams were driftin',
Ne'er win up tae the hills fan the mist was liftin',
   Nor hark tae the sooth win's sang.

Doon the loanin' an' up the close
   The fite-harled hoose is waitin' me;
Ay, yon's the hame far my weary banes should bide,
Far couthily I micht sit by the trig fireside
   Nor fash aboot hills or sea.

But its doon the close an' up the loanin',
   For, oh, the road rins bonnily;
An' e'en though the ebb-tide bears my dreams awa',
E'en though the nor' win' smores the hills in sna',
   I'll haud tae the road till I dee.

(1931)

By David Cairns

I KNOW THAT SOON MY JOURNEY WILL BE DONE

I know that soon my journey will be done;
I'm grateful that though dulling of my sense
Has crept upon me, still a joy immense
Comes from sheer mountains standing in the sun,
Delphinium spikes in iridescent bloom,
And from the morning radiance in a room;
For though my body's old and worn and ill,
My heart and mind are like a young man's still.
May my way hence be under friendly skies,
Set free from weakness and my crippling bond,
The wind upon my brow, my heart once more
Startled by joy, my body's energies
Able to crest the ridges as before,
To reach the peak, and O! what lies beyond!

(1990)

SONG

Wherever I wander, these woods shall be dear,
Where the snowdrop comes first at the turn o' the year,
Where the oak and the pine grow, and red-clustered rowan,
O west wind, blaw lichtly on lovely Blawlowan.

Oft there hae we listened, my Jessie and I,
To the laverock's song in the evening sky,
And the sough o' the wind, and the clear burnie rowin';
O west wind, blaw lichtly on lovely Blawlowan.

Tho' aften hae Logie's woods laucht tae the spring,
Syne ower the wide sea I gaed wandering,
Yet as merle tae its nest, and the dew tae the gowan,
So will I return to the lass o' Blawlowan.

(1989)

SCOTLAND IN EARLY SUMMER

O lovely land of quilted fields and farms
Where the wild rose in tender beauty blooms.
Above, there float delicate galleons of the clouds,
And blue hills frame the horizon.
May God be with you and my countrymen!

(1990)

By W M Calder

LAUDATIO FUNEBRIS – OLD STYLE

Hic sita est Amymone Marci optima et pulcherrima lanifica pia pudica frugi casta domiseda.

C. I. L., vi, 11602.

> Here lies Rob Allan's bonny Bell,
>   A tenty dame,
> That span her 'oo', an' said her prayers,
>   An' bade at hame.

(1921)

By Agnes C Carnegie

TODESERFAHRUNG
FROM THE GERMAN OF RAINER MARIA RILKE

Death is inscrutable and keeps his state
beyond us while we live; and yet, unwise,
we look on him with wonder, love or hate,
death that appears to us in strange disguise

wearing the mourning mask of tragedies.
The world has parts to play for everyone;
and, while we care for little but to please,
death plays his too, although he pleases none.

But when you died a shaft of radiance streamed
across this stage where you had broken through
to reach reality; and what had seemed
then truly was, true forest, sunlight true.

We go on playing; parts we learned with pain
and careless reciting, page by page,
making a pregnant gesture now and then;
but from your being, rapt beyond our stage,

come to us hints of that reality
that through the crack in radiance came pouring,
so that, transported for a while, we play
our parts in very truth, applause ignoring.

(1949)

15

By William Christie

AN UNCO HAIRST
(Mains o' Bogandreep Soliloquises)

Ay, Man, that's a braw hairst day the day,
    An' troth, it's nae afore time;
For an unco hairst we've haen – they say
    It's the warst sin' '99.
Never a day but the rain's dung doon
    An' sypit an' laid the corn;
Yon park i' the best o' the grun intoon –
    I'll be glad gin it war shorn.
I'll need the scythes doon fae the laft,
    The binder couldn'a dee't –
Forbye, the grun'll be far ower saft
    For the wecht o' the horses' feet.
An' the twa-three sheaves that I hae got bun'
    Are blackenin' at the heid,
An' I sair misdoot, gin the grain war grun'
    There'll be a gey 'nip' i' the breid.
The tatties are rottin' ootbye' i' the dreels,
    They'll be connacht, or I'm mislippent sair,
For ilka day stans the weet in peels
    An' the lift aye dings doon mair.
It's nae gweed kennin' fat a body sud dee
    An' sna' i' the hills already;
For the kye'll need maet an' the men their fee
    For they've tyuavt and wrocht rael steady.
It disna sair to grane an' girn
    We just maun mak' the best o't;
Fat eese a load abeen a birn?
    We'll yoke an' scythe the rest o't.

(1956)

FROM SAPPHO

δέδυκε μὲν ἀ σελάννα
καὶ πληῖαδες, μέσαι δέ
νύκτες, παρὰ δ'ἔρχετ' ὥρα,
ἔγω δὲ μόνα κατεύδω.

The meen's awa, the Sisters set,
The mid hour o' the nicht has gane,
But, O, my Laddie comesna yet,
An' dowff I lie my leeve-alane.

(1963)

16

By Ivo M Clark

ATWEEN THE GLOAMIN' AN THE MIRK
(TO THE ARTS CLASS, 1901–05)

Near fifty years sin doon the Spittal brae
    We gaed in anes or twas that fatefu' day,
Fan first we met at King's, and Clerk and Dean
    Determined fa wad burs'ries get, fa neen,
Jist loons an lassies fae the kintra skweel
    Produc's o hame an pedagogic zeal.
Fae Dee an Don, the Broch and Foggieloan,
    Fae Manse hine up the glen an skweelhouse lone,
Fae fushin village frontin oonquate seas,
    Fae bonnie howes wi fairm-toons hod in trees,
Fae Hielan craft an uplan Banffshire fairm,
    Cam lads an lasses unca keen tae learn
An drink deep drauchts o the Pierian spring,
    Thirstin' for that abeen a' ither thing;
An nae a fyou fae Aiberdeen itsel
    At h'ard abeen its din the College bell.
We spak the tongues o a' the Nations fower,
    Saft Gaelic speech 'at wis the Celtic dower,
The couthie Doric, mither tongue o maist,
    An antrin ane at English did his best.

An sae begood that life aneth the Croon,
    Ower brief tae ane that's worn the auld reid goon,
Ae day like poppy i' the caul grey street,
    The morn it's gane – tae min' on't gars ye greet.
The Kin'ly Mither gaithered in her brood,
    A fell oonrowly, contermachious crood;
A kittle job tae lick them intil shape,
    Bit she haed weys na ither Nurse cud ape,
A ban' o nurses male at her comman',
    Tho human a', they plied the heavy han',
Ha'wa, Billy, an auld Charlie Niven,
    Gweed teachers a', neen better under heaven,
Bourtie an Baillie an Grierson, Terry, Trail –
    the lad tae catch the early mornin' snail –
Peerie at startit aff his class wi prayer,
    An Airthur Tamson wi his gowden hair;
The potters they, an we bit dauds o clay
    Furl'd on the wheel they ca'd baith nicht an day,
Niz glu'd tae buik or scrattin eident pen
    Tae preeve nae thing there wis we didna ken.
If leevin plain an thinkin heich cud mak
    For fame an gear, we sud hae kent nae lack;
The calories an veetamines we nott
    We beet tae fin' them i' the parritch pot.

Gey dreich were digs, tho foster-mithers kin'
  Tae lichtsome callant or tae hame-sick quine,
An, man, fan Yeeltide cam, sic byous bustle,
  An hame an neepers wi the ingin's fussle!
Noo motor-cars an bikes thrang a' the Quad,
  Tae hurl ye tae yer wark an back, peer lad,
For hiz shank's naig tae King's or bawbee tram;
  An foreneen coffee? jist a scone an jam!
Nae chaiplain fash'd his sowl tae save us a',
  We gaed tae Chaipel or we bade awa;
Nae Doc tae luik oor tongue or tak oor wecht
  Or stick on plaister at a peasemeal fecht.
Some fitba played, at shinty ithers bled,
  Cursin the fae in Gaelic (sae 'twis said).
Bit tho, tell't no in Gath, Carnegie fees
  First cam oor wey and gied a hantle ease
Tae pooches near-han teem, we still an on
  Haed ploys, class supper, shine or cairry-on,
An aft the lift abeen a Rosemount street
  Wad ring wi throaty sang, an steyterin feet
Wad gang bi Ferryhill tae see ane hame
  At sud hae been at Robsla a' the same.
We grat, we leuch, we swat, an we *d.p.*'d,   (duly performed)
  An ane or twa jist dwein'd awa and dee'd;
A wat, the three-fower year gaed by ower seen,
  For some o's never haed oor dargs half-deen;
The Profs, wi ootside help, fair screen'd us a';
  Tho' maist o's got degrees, some neen ava,
A fyou wi harns or ingine tae tak pains
  Were capp'd wi Honours an took a' the gains.
An syne wi braw fite hoods slung roon oor necks
  Fat mair tae dee, we thocht, than lift the snecks
An walk richt intil a' the ha's o fame
  An keep on addin letters till oor name?

   · · · · · · · · · · · ·

The Class haed skail'd, the faimly broken up,
  Baith fast and feast were ower, an teem the cup.
The feck had santit clean awa, as burn
  Tae sea, as reek tae clood, withoot return,
Binna a fyou like wraiths aboot the Quad
  'At still haed houps some mair degrees tae add
Tae gie them poo'er tae cure a' fleshly ills,
  Pluck burnin bran's, or draw up codicils.
Wi a's degrees the hinmaist set his face
  The wey the ithers gaed fan on the race
O life they yokit, bi the Spital brae,
  Mounthoolie an the Gallagate sae grey,
The street ca'd Broad (as braid's the road tae hell
  An fu' o promise like the Mairrage Bell),

That led sae mony far ayont the faem,
   (Tho' some bade still, gey siccar, nearer hame)
Tae ilka Continent, baith aist an wast,
   Tae Africa an mony a farrer cast
They gaed, an seen they were at grips wi Fate
   An for mishanters hadna lang tae wait.

   · · · · · · · · · · · ·

In time douce merriet fowk wi bairns an hame,
   A job tae dee an wi less thocht o fame,
Jist peace an quate aifter youth's waukrife age
   Tae think a fyle an syne turn ower a page,
Bit, losh keeps a', that's nae the wey things gang,
   An gi'ein nae a snuff for vricht or vrang,
The Kaiser thocht wi Truth tae brak a lance
   An pour'd his Huns intil the hert o' France.
An in the war 'at wis tae en' a' war,
   Dubbit wi glory an wi Flanders glaur,
Bajans o Nineteen-Ane, like vet'rans teuch,
   Swore, 'Damn'd be him at first cries, Haud, eneuch.'

   · · · · · · · · · · · ·

Syne fan the lave wun hame an roll wis ta'en,
   – It min's ye o' the tale o Cairnaquheen –
Upo' the cairn 'at haed begood tae rise
   Aucht steens were laid tae mark the sacrifice
O seaven at sleep in graves a' poppy-deck'd,
   An ane 'at lies in Adriatic wreck'd.

Cam on the lang ooneasy years atween
   The wars, an eident – noo 'twis aifterneen –
We socht tae sattle tae the wark in han',
   Bit, man alive, like sheen a' fu o san',
Disjaskit were oor min's year aifter year
   By *putsch* abroad or things a' oot o gear
At hame; a fell camsteerie byous time
   O *demarche*, collieshangie, crisis, crime;
We tchaav'd awa, wi a' the warl gane gyte,
   Jalousin sair faur it wad en', Awyte.
It didna mak ava foo hard we vrocht
   The haill hypothec till a stop wis brocht,
Fan Nazi hordes ower Europe *berserk* gaed,
   An a' oor bits o schemes in ruin laid.

   · · · · · · · · · · · ·

Some o's were first tae jine the L.D.V.;
   An ithers wan their spurs in A.R.P.,
Creepin ower reefs or burrowin' i' the yird
   An hame tae bed wi sang o early bird.
That life, sair fashed wi twa or three men's wark,
   Forbye aye noo an than some dreedit yark –
– Ill news o son or some weel-likit loon
   'At wad nae mair come in aboot the toon –

Tyeuk toll sae heavy o oor thinnin' line
　We grue tae think on't as it wis lang syne.
　　. . . . .

Fat div we think o't a', this tchaav ca'd life,
　That's been the lot o's a', baith man and wife?
It's nae for hiz tae yammer an compleen
　Or greet aboot the things 'at micht hae been.
We did the best we cud; 'weel, weel' say they,
　(They haif said, Quhat say they, E'en lat yame say).
They've dubbit neen o's Sir; there cam oor wey
　An LL.D. or twa, an by the bye
A D.D. tee, an feint a muckle mair
　Bit medals in a box ablow the stair.
Did life turn oot tae be the gran' success
　Dream'd o', fan we gaed doon, an Girdleness
Reel'd far ahin? Fa kens, we speir, fa kens?
　Tae answer that wad weer doon mony pens.
The Chanc'llor haes the last wird at the gate;
　He kens oor marks; lat's houp He'll cap oor pate
Honoris causa-wise, withoot exam,
　For noo it's far ower late tae try an cram.
We've haed oor chance, Gweed kens, tae live an lairn –
　The steens are pilin' fester on the cairn.

　　　　　　　　　　　　　　　　　　　(1950)

20

By John Cook

THE SMITH

We aivened oot the twistit thraws,
  An' syne his een we steikit:
The corp, till Leebie dressed his braws,
  Aside the laith we streikit.

Fu' waefu' frae the shoein' fleer
  We raised his buirdly frame:
Deil tak the nag wha's lichtnin huiv
  Was yarkit in his wame.

Here's airn for a cadger's hake,
  And there's a new-laid coulter,
An' Howie's broken reaper-rake
  Sits bi' the auld wife's pooter.

Nae mair we'll see the evenin' lowe
  Lichtin' his stoury baird:
Nae mair he'll rest the bellows han'
  An crack wi' hind an' herd.

Bi' noo he's stowfin' blithely up
  The gowden, starry stair:
He'll tak his graith again, an' men'
  The trumps wi' meikle care.

(1931)

By Elizabeth Craigmyle

ON THE EVENING OF A FUNERAL
(W. B. G. MINTO, 5 July, 1919.)

'Peace hath her victories as renowned as War.'
  Peace hath her sombre tragedy as well:
  He bore a charmed life through the shot and shell,
Gallant and gay, insouciant; not a scar,
('Not even a scratch!' said laughing,) when afar
  He fought, and now some hideous miracle
  Has brought an end like this, – the passing bell,
The men he loved following a flag-draped car.

Strange silly trifles come from memory's store,
  As I recall a schoolboy's bright, brown eyes,
  Evenings with story-books, stamps, butterflies,
And far, far off, – O weird, impossible thing!
(Not for the soldier is my heart so sore)
A little child that used to kiss and cling.

(1920)

By David Daiches

BALCONIES

A balcony is the best suspension.
High above pavement we command the scene;
Secure, serene, on our wrought-iron stand
We raise our glasses. Summer evening drinks
Are best on balconies. But there are other uses,
Other pleasures, other dangers.
Juliet had her balcony and many a lover
Has climbed to one or scrambled down from one,
And many a lonely scholar
Has leant on a balcony rail, sadly observing.
I have seen balconies
In Edinburgh's New Town,
Douce, quietly respectable, no mad escapes
From there or lovers' leaps. Mediterranean balconies
In courtyards, or outside bedroom windows towards the sea.
How many scenes in film or theatre
Have linked the balcony to deeds of passion,
Actions of high romance.

But I remember
Sipping an evening grappa on a balcony
In Genoa with you while the storm raged
And lightning lit the sky.
I see it now a symbol of our life
Together, suspended in mutual love,
Facing a raging world.
Now you are gone I look for balconies,
Symbols of lost content.

(1992)

By Elizabeth T Dawson

THE MICHT-HAE-BEEN

She sits her lane bi the canle licht
an' thinks on the micht-hae-been:
an' a weel-faured lad comes ben til her
wi' the love-lowe in his een.

She sees the hoose an' the pangit press,
an' a twa-three bairns at play;
an' their lauchter thirls her wearie hert
lik a sun-glaff winter's day.

She's taen a silk goon frae the kist
an' slippit it owre her heid:
though it wisna nott bi a jinkit bride
it'll set her brawlie deid.

She sits her lane throwe the lang forenicht
an' mines on the micht-hae-been:
bit the fire burns dowie in her breist,
an' the canle's a bit deen.

(1953)

24

By Hunter Diack

THE WHITE SPACES

The problem now is to find the white spaces.
For, as education marches into the waste land,
the words agglutinate
and leave little space between them
for the ideas to grow.
So the problem now is to find the white spaces.

The problem is complicated by the fact that now
too many writers too often
spoil the white spaces
with marks they take to be words.

Before an answer can be found,
it is necessary to find the question,
but it does not follow that if the question is not found,
there is no answer.
This is a simple way of declaring that a problem may exist
without its existence being known –
such as the problem of finding the spaces
when the writer himself may not have known,
though he thought he was writing words,
he was merely spoiling the spaces.

The spoiling of spaces is like the dripping of water
on the stone of truth.
With each occurrence there is a change,
and here the change is
that the distinction
between the space that is spoilt and the word
is blurred.
That is to say,
the brain is no longer able
with ease to make the distinction
between spoilt space
and valid word.

A further difficulty arises
when, as so often occurs,
the spoilers of spaces
think they are engaged on the task
of keeping clear the distinction
between the word and the space,
for when they have spoilt enough spaces,
the problem of distinguishing between word and space
disappears,

but only because we have lost
awareness of difference.

The world we live in is a series of illusions,
for nothing is as we see it now
but only as our senses read it
in the context of what has gone before.
There is no seeing without interpretation
and all interpretation is incomplete;
so nothing is known but always about to be known.

To live in the fixed belief
that the Thing is what our senses show it to be
is a mode of insanity,
but this is the mode of education,
which drills its victims in the fiction
that the Thing *is* what our senses show it to be.

To declare that reality is not what our senses show it to be
is not to deny that reality is what it is,
but merely to deny our final knowing.
To do that is to move towards sanity.

It can be accepted that man,
with his hindsight and foresight,
his holding of concepts,
his levels of abstraction,
may move on a higher plane than the animals.
But that he should do so is not a necessity.

A trout cannot refuse to swim,
nor an eagle to fly;
that is their truth.
But man does not of necessity
accept the truth of his nature.
Inventive, he creates fictions
and, debauched by the spoilers of spaces,
drifts into thinking them truths.

I am asking you then
to set aside knowledge of Things
and cultivate awareness of processes,
for this is the way of freedom
from the rigidity imposed by education.

You are, then, not to regard the mountains as stable,
or the sky as blue,
for you know that in this past-becoming moment –
faith neither here nor there, –
the mountains have moved;

you must know too that the sky,
black when you reach the end of air,
is a play of light as on a one-way screen.
It is necessary, therefore, that your brain must tell you
that you cannot believe
what your brain tells you your eyes have seen.

I am asking you, then,
to set aside knowledge of Things
and cultivate awareness of processes.

That which we call a Thing,
even a Thing-in-itself,
is a series of processes;
and the Word,
conceived as the name of the Thing
is no less a series of processes.
The processes that are the Thing
are the outer processes;
those that are the Word
are the inner;
The confusing of outer and inner processes
is a mode of insanity;
but education,
hallucinative,
works on the assumption
that the name of the inner process
is the name of the outer – the Thing,
and so retreats from sanity.

(1989)

THE SIGNPOST

ERROGIE – *4 miles.*
Chance walked with me across the heather
and brought me to that sign-post.
I paused, thought, felt,
and chose another road,
yet stood by that earth's magnet fixed
till he drove up who said,
'You're bound for Errogie?'
I shook my head, 'Not there.'
'Gorthlech, maybe, or Inverfarigaig?'
Tombreck or Farr?'
'It might, it might be one of those
and yet I'm going nowhere particular.'
'That's odd.' He scratched his chin.
'Why odd? Surely a man may walk
just walk, without a thought
of reaching any place that has a name.'
'Of course,' he said. 'That's not the oddness.'
'All right, you tell me where the oddness lies.'
'If you are going nowhere particular,
you should be going anywhere at all,
but you've cut out the place called Errogie,
so can't be going anywhere at all.'
'So that's the oddness is't,' I said.
'It's odder still to meet a casuist
here at the back of this beyond.'
'I thought to be a priest,' he said.
'They threw me out. I asked too many questions.
Let's put it down to that.'
'And where are you now heading for?
Where does the end of your road lie?'
'Right here,' he said, 'at least for the time being.'
I looked around at empty miles.
'There's beauty here,' I said, 'and peace,
as good a place to stop as anywhere at all.'
'No doubt,' he said,
'but I've got work to do. Right here.
The sign-post needs a lick of paint
and that's my job.'
'Then you'll go on to paint more sign-posts
to Gorthlech, maybe, and Inverfarigaig,
Tombreck and Farr?'
'And Dunmaglass,' he added,
he who'd thought to sign-post folk to heaven.
'I expect you know these places well.'

He shook his head.
'I'd not say that. I've never felt the need
to know the places I paint sign-posts to.'
Nor did I feel the need to tell him
that to me his sign-post lied.
For me there was no road to Errogie
nor tallied miles.
The Errogie I'd heard of, never knew,
lay light-years back
among the tumbled hills
beyond the Celtic twilight
where time was purple when it was not gold,
where birch-leaves in a net of light
above the trembling waters hung.
'I hope you'll come to Errogie
some day,' the letter said.
I did not go
and now the one who asked me then
has gone – nowhere particular,
but not, I think, anywhere at all
just some where, some place
where sign-posts need no painting
and point to nowhere particular.

Errogie – four miles.
There it stood
at the end that is the beginning
of all the roads I did not take
but might have taken,
of all the paths I did not tread,
but might have trodden,
and they stretch further
than all the roads and paths I've travelled
on foot on wheel or in mind,
alack and well away beyond
Gorthlech and Inverfarigaig,
Tombreck or Farr.

(1991)

29

By Alexander R Dow

PROVOST DAVIDSON AND THE HEROES OF HARLAW
(Toast proposed at St Andrew's Society of Aberdeen dinner on
30 November 1976)

Guid people tak tent, for there must cam amangst ye this day
The memory o' a company o' richt redoubtit knechts, the whilk,
Hath not been in these airts full mony a year.
Within your heids, project ye forrit, half a millenium wi
Saxty and five years mair, from fourteen hundert and eleven, that
    summer sair
Tae this year 1976, of grace. Think on't what micht dare,
Donald, Lord o the Isles, tae traverse North Caledonia
And invest this citie fair, Aberdeen on the Germane Sea.

Grant that, all that lang, lang syne, Donald was sair aggreivit,
Though cousin tae the Earl o Mar, he was ootna wedlock sirit,
As Bastard son o Badenoch's Wolf, unseemly dispossessit
Of his, or his wife's claim to Ross' Earldom, – thievit
By Albany, Scotland's Regent, who all that fief translatit
Tae his ain son, the Earl o Buchan.

Grant that this, Donald rousit. Whae casts on him the blame.
But what, in 1976, would rouse him, just the same,
Tae march upon this fair citie wi clamour, and adversitie?
Would it be sparseness o' the fish that flee from oot the Minches flow,
Or English lairds on Rathsay's Isle, where indecorum warps the lives
Of croftin folk?

Grant that he micht ravage Ross, and cross to make foray,
With battle here or skirmish there, first with Celt then Lowlander
And on to douce Moray.
Gie him pause in wild Strathspey, tae gape and glower,
At cheirs suspendit from a rope, that swing and sway and trail chiels
    ower,
The very heid o' Cairngorm – investit aye wi sna' late on.
Or watch entrancit muckle beasts that hiss and snort
And doon an iron track, strauchter than any cairters' road,
That ever Hieland man has seen, thirty or forty waggon loads, all
    destined doon tae Aberdeen.

Then ower Corsemaul, his horde would pour, still fou o' ravage and
    rapine
Strathbogie, then through Foundlands Glen – and tae the Sooth, fair
    Benachie,
Tae Harlaw field, there, stock tae tak, for still near twenty miles from
    Aberdeen.
Now, in that Toon, what lodestone draw, micht tryst ten thoosand
    Hielander

Its granite quarries scrattit bare, baith grey and reed, nae stane, now
    left owerturnit,
And herrin drifters fast in Port, Icelandic forays thwartit.
Dispersit through the Toon, mair hostelries tae serve three hundred
    thousand thrapples dry
Mair than the Shiprow Tabard Inn where Sir Robt. Davidson,
Played host to but three thousand souls o populace. A Provost who
    wrocht, Innkeeper
Exciseman, Factor for King and Gentrie, Merchant, Customs man
    forbye,
And in the Borough Court who pled with douce felicity. Heid Burgher in
A Toon where now, hot watter rins frae pipes at a screw's turn,
Leviathanic wagons fell up and doon, and highways burn
Frae here to Europe, furth awa than oor Shore Porters Wagons
Waxit forth eighty-three years ahent Harlaw
Na'ne o' these things, but in this year, could stand sae high wi oil.
'Oil' that name which, if one peruse the great new Lexicon o Scottish
    words
Descrivit thus, – 'Black, skity, liquid, glaury tar, that springs
Furth ootna ground or leich uneath the Germane Sea – spoots and
Drawn forth by spinnin augurs, mountit, hexapoddit, tetrapoddit,
    skites astride the waves,
Like a great Colossus. They twist and rug their way through ocean's fleer
Or crust Earth to depths afore unfathomable.
Oil tae poor on troublit watters. Gaur stiff joints swacken and ungeal.
To rin explodit in a hollow tube, fired and ignitit by a spark,
That drives a wheel roon at a rate eneuch tae pit the fear o' mortal
Hell – into the very Deil himsel'.

So, like this year, when Burghers still nae fear would show,
To march ootbye tae Harlaw field, so, – back to Garioch,
Fourteen hundert and eleven when Davidson, his Burghers and all
    they held in thrall
Marched oot wi' all the Gentrie roondaboot, frae Buchan,
Formartine, Strathbogie roon and Mar. Names, the very soond of
    which
Must race the pulsin bleed o' all who call this Citie – 'Hame'.
Hark to these names,
Alex Irvine, Laird o' Drum
Gilbert o Greenlaw
James Scrymgeour, Constable o' Dundee.
Abernethy o' Saltoun
Robert Maul Panmure
Sir Alex Straiton of Lauriston
Leslie o' Balquhain
(and he deit not alane, but wi six sons, his very ain)
Tullidaff, – o' Lenteish and Rothmais
Forbes, Stewarts, Gordons, Keiths
Burnets, Lindsays, Frasers, Leiths.
All who perishit that day.

So, brief before the minutes pass, and silence on you all shall fall,
Hark to the sound o' battle focht, a century before Harlaw
For baith sounds, this day or then, it's all the same for those
Who Saxon Knecht or Celtish be, tis all the same adversitie,
If Death be the calamitie.

John Barbour: *The Battle o' Bannockburn*
There was the battle stricken weill;
So great dinnin there was of dyntis
As wapyns upon great armpur stintis,
And of spearis so great bristing
With sic thrawing and sic thrusting,
Sic girning, granyng, and so great
A noise, as they can other beat,
And cryit ensenyeis on everilk side,
Gifand and takand woundis wide,
That it was hideous for till hear.
Fechtand in till ae front wholly
Almichty God, full douchtely
Fechtand into sa good covyne
So hardy worthy and so fine
That their avaward rushit was
And maugre theiris left the place,
And to their great rout to warrand
They went that then had upon hand
So great not that they were effrayit
For Scottis men them hard assayit
That then war in ane shiltrom all
Wha happnit in that ficht to fall
I trow again he suld not rise
There men micht see on mony wise
Hardiment eschevit douchtely
And mony that wicht were and hardy
Doun under feet lyand all dede
Whar all the field of blood was red
Armouris and quyntis that they bare
With blood was swa defoulit there
That they might nocht descrivit be.

So wrote Barbour o' Bannockburn ane hundred years afore Harlaw,
So was it then and so must now, ye all stand,
And let your heids doon fa'
– And in your quietude,
Think weel o' Provost Davidson and ALL the Heroes o' Harlaw.

(1977)

32

By Ronald Draper

MEMORIAL
For Roger O'Donovan: Garthlock 7 July 1991

We cannot touch the dead;
Their peace is sealed and delivered
To whatever address the wind has blown their ashes.
If we stand among newly-planted trees,
Ground sodden, the mid-day sun fiercely disinterested,
To celebrate the digger, it is not to be fooled
By Feste or by festivities,
But to cool the blaze of a pain that beats on us.
Death is a game we play quite seriously,
We live by its laws and are ruled
By its rules as a salmon its source
Slithering back on the rocks that we know we must climb.
Afterwards wake to the world,
Mix in relief with its meshes,
And die to the sun. Barkis is willing:
Elegies are for the living.

(1992)

33

By John Elwolde

MAWTU FILFARANDJ
(Death in the West)

Your fountains now are dry
Who in Andalusia reigned
To sand once more return
The memories of a caliph past
Her libraries lie bare
Burned down or serving God in France
Cordova's mental wealth
Transferred to Paris Toledo
With Ibn Rushd and alchemy
And those like you who soon will kill
Ha-Levi and his seed
Employment give as targomans
So snakish wend you thence
As subtlety in spite sublimes.

(1986)

By Alice M M Farquhar

APRIL DAY

Slim birches clasped in silver, white clouds above the hills,
The willows' golden fringes, and foam on dancing rills,
The green of budding larches, the heather wine and grey,
But no one here beside me to mark the sparkling day.

The swan upon the ripples, the dabchick in the weeds,
The sunshine on the river, the wind across the reeds,
The woodman's yellow plunder, the hillside's ravaged scar,
But no one here to notice the snow on Lochnagar.

No eyes to match with laughter the gladness of the fields,
No heart to note how swiftly grim winter's army yields,
No voice to welcome springtime to hill and loch and tree,
No tranquil friendly presence to share the world with me.

(1949)

By A S Ferguson

CASIDA OF THE BRANCHES
(Translated from the Spanish of FEDERICO LORCA)

Up and down the woods of Tamarit
Now the pack of leaden hounds have come,
And wait to see the branches falling down,
And wait to see them dropping of themselves.

By Tamarit there stands an apple-tree,
And from that tree a sobbing apple hangs;
A nightingale to gather up the sighs,
A pheasant-cock to chase them through the dust.
But the branches are light-hearted;
But the branches are like us.
Not a thought for the rain; they're sound asleep,
Behaving like the great trees, off at once.

Tranquil, knee-deep in their quiet water
Two valleys wait and watch for autumn.
Trampling like an elephant, the Shadow
Loom'd, and shouldered bough and bole aside.

Up and down the woods of Tamarit
Range troops of boys with muffled faces,
And wait to see the branches falling down,
And wait to see them dropping of themselves.

(1939)

36

By Olive Fraser

THE DIPPER'S NEST THAT OVERHANGS THE RIVER NAIRN

Pass by most quietly this quiet nest
But keep it like a jewel in thy breast.
It and its bright inhabitant will save
Thee from some grave.

Her care, her watchful silence shall stay nigh
To comfort thee when thirty years go by.
Thou shalt take strength amid some deadly strife
From this hid life.

There is some vestige of divinity
Fast plaited here upon a long-branched tree
Above a stream. Some hour this nest will come
To seem thy home.

(1976)

THE KING'S STUDENT

All men do sleep in night and darkness dead
Save thee, Callimachus, reading in bed.
Thy windy candle lights a page, a part,
But a great, crownéd lantern lights thy heart.

(1946)

By R J B Garden

THE LOST WINE
(After Paul Valéry)

> Into the ocean, one fine day,
> (Under what skies I can't now guess),
> All my precious wine I poured away,
> An offering to nothingness.
>
> Precious liquid, who desired your loss?
> Did I obey a call divine?
> Perhaps I felt my own heart toss,
> Dreaming in the blood, spilling the wine.
>
> Their old transparence the waves at last,
> After the rosy smoke had passed,
> Resumed as pure, as clear, as fair.
>
> The wine was lost, drunk was the sea,
> But I saw leap in the bitter air
> Figures of great profundity.

(1994)

By Flora Garry

THE CAT
(Freely translated from Baudelaire's *Les Fleurs du Mal*)

My big, browe cat-beast, croose an' tame,
Stravaigin roun' my parlour fleer,
In my min's benmost nyeuk, I'll sweir,
Ye've fun yersel' a second hame.

Fyles ye myurr-myurr to me my leen,
Yer trimmlin myowies syne sae sma'
An' saft they're fint a soun' ava.
Ye're couthy fan in fraizin teen.

But fyles yer birss begoods to rise
An' rummlins fae yer thrapple birl
Wi' fearsome gurr an' feerious dirl
Like thunner rivin simmer skies.

An' fan, ower-laid wi' warldly care,
I dwine in dark despondency,
Ye'll come, my cat, an' purr tae me,
Yer three-threids-an'-a-thrum I'll hear.

An' syne my dolour's heavy fraacht
Growes licht, yer sangie warms my veins
Like some aul' ballant's liltin strains
Or like a love-brew's heidy draacht.

I've h'ard fiddle-tunes sae rare
An' sweet they'd thowe a hert o' steen
An' fire the caul'est bleed, but neen
Wi' yours, my Bawdrons, can compare.

Ye're a dumb brute, nae wirds hiv ye,
Yet a' the joys by Man e'er pree'd
Your tongue can tell; na, ye've nae need
To speel a lang langamachie.

An ootlin fae some idder warl',
A speerit-craitur, keerious,
Oonchancy, fey, mysterious
To me, a feel, roch human carl.

This hoose is yours, the gear, the folk,
Ootside an' in, baith but an' ben,
Its sowle, its reet an' rise ye ken.
Are ye a god or deevilock?

I min', ae nicht, fan straikin ye,
Yer coat o' yalla tortyshell
Ceest on the air sic balmy smell
Its sweet reek yoamt a' ower me.

To watch ye is a richt divert,
My een as by a lodesteen draan.
Siccar ye grip me, an' I'm thraan
To turn to my ain thochts, to pairt

Fae you. But still an' on I'll see,
In my min's benmost nyeuk, I'll sweir,
Like bleezin cwyles o' caul' green fire,
Your twa een glowerin' straacht at me.

(1952)

SUTHERLAND STREET, W.2

A far, far cry to Sutherland Street
From moor and loch, seal on the wave-washed rock,
Stag on the hill and eagle in the cloud
And sunset's benediction on the Hebrides.
From Assynt and Benmore, from Eriboll,
Far indeed to the street called Sutherland.

Here the beetling man-made tenement cliffs,
Hewn and chiselled mountain caricatures.
Here the cylindrical peaks of chimney-pots.
Window-gullies, geometric slits,
Like unseeing eyes reject the leaden light.
From close-mouths, as from caves, the people pass
Along the pavement's rigid valley-floor.
Shaped like the clothes of the better multiple stores
In the advertisement pages of magazines,
They have pale, withdrawn faces and the look,
Guarded and wary, of the hurt or hunted beast.
They are the comfortable middle-class,
Who have never known bodily hunger or stress.
A few will leave to their heirs some small estate.
All have carefully conditioned minds,
Moulded by school and university,
Cinema, lending library, radio.
They think in slogans and in cliché phrases.
They love their class and their respectability.
For an ideology they will fight and die.
Of the line of martyrs, saints and fanatics,

40

They are civilization's finest flower,
Who daily tread the drab front steps of Sutherland Street.
Now daily they must walk with fear for friend,
With black misgiving seeks their beds each night,
The fabric of their dreaming interwoven
With dread of future insecurity.
Such is the northern aspect of the street,
Chill, repellent and impenetrable
Fortress of inviolate gentility.
But look with me from my high window down
On the yards, the back doors and the drying greens.
Look on the southern aspect of the street.
Here stand the dust-bins and the air-raid shelters.
Here are trodden earth and sour grass.
A woman carries a bucket full of ashes.
The garments she wears are work-stained, nondescript.
Clumsy, slow is her dateless female form,
Fashioned by toil and childbirth down the ages.
Moving between the flat-roofed, hut-like shelters,
She is a figure from the dawn of history.
She tilts the dust-bin lid, the grimy zinc
Is harsh beneath her finger-tips, the wind
Swirls the gritty ashes between her teeth.
Here is physical labour, the ebb and flow
Of seasonal cold and heat, of growth and flower;
The new gold of laburnum buds in May
On old and sooty boughs, a dandelion
Shining from a brick wall in July.
Here a young man, whistling, mends a chair,
A young wife hangs her baby-clothes to dry.
Windows are opened, curtains billow out.
Neuter cats sleep curled on sunny sills.
A man in shirt-sleeves washes at a sink.
A woman reads and sips a cup of tea.
A girl at a mirror gravely paints her lips
And music blares from a dozen wireless sets.
This, then, is the back of Sutherland Street.
This is natural man, who loves his home,
His children and his ease; creature of instinct
And of appetite, compelled even now
By natural laws and force of circumstance,
Moulded still by his environment.
But see him stepping down from his front door,
Precisely gloved and hatted, wary-eyed.
Here is Man become Mind, the architect
And builder of his own environment,
Bewildered and appalled by his own creation,
Fearful of his self-appointed destiny.

Perhaps when 'the time of the breaking of the nations' is ended,
And life renews itself amid the ruins,
In some far corner, Eriboll maybe,
Or Assynt or Benmore, there will arise
A huddle of stone-built huts. – The night draws on.
A woman, stooping, stirs with a knotty branch
Ashes and sparks from a fire on the bare ground.
A man sits, crouching low, beside the flames.
His look is withdrawn, intent, his whole being
Centred in the motions of his fingers.
With fragments of bone and wood he has made a hook,
A fishing hook, a new and better hook.
The eagle seeks her nest on the jutting crag,
The stag in the grassy hollow makes his bed,
The seal slips seaward on the ebbing tide
And sunset, lingering, gilds the Hebrides.
But man, with his fishing hook, is on the road
That winds through centuries of growth and toil,
 Frustration, exultation, agony,
 And brings him home at last – we wonder where –
 Not, we pray, to a second Sutherland Street.

(1951)

BOG COTTON

Pick and discard if you will
Bluebell and daffodil.
They must pay for your holiday.
Let them unheeded lie
Under heel or wheel,
Or let them die
Untended in the jar upon the window-sill.

Or make a casual posy
Of buttercup and daisy,
Honey-suckle, pansy,
Purple vetch and tansy,
Roadside flowers expendable,
Familiar, plain and cosy.

But lay no vandal finger on that flower-wraith,
Bog-cotton, whitening on the winds of June
In solitary places where the curlew pipes.
Wan and chill its flaring candle-flames
Illumine the high altar of the moor.
Those pale fires swept the wastes of the antique world
When thaw struck off earth's icy manacles.
They knew the strange green twilight of the brooding tundra.
Rooted in raw peat, fed by the alchemy
Of subsidence, compression, sun and rain,
Their feet are set where once the lordly heads
Of oak and pinetree tossed in the salty gales
Blown from the young estranging northern sea
Over the ancient forest lands of Caledon.
They knew the circling stone, the priest at his rites,
The hymn to the stars, the blood of the cockerel.

Leave uncontaminate the little torches,
Leave that fleeting magic to the wind's cold breath.
No comfort here for man in his mortality.
Tread with apprehension when you walk the moors.

(1959)

By Arthur Geddes

THE BRIG O' BALGOWNIE
Air, traditional

My luve sae lang, this day we'll gang
  ow'r the deeps o' the flowing Don,
Our tryst be the rig o' the ae-span Brig
  o' Balgownie ow'r the Don.

We'll win our way, dear lass, the day,
  where you turned to me, fain an' fon',
Seal troth at the Mairch where the poynted airch
  ow'rspans the darklin' Don.

Frae bank to bank sae steep and dank,
  it rises til the sun:
Sae, groyne by groyne, our brig shall joyne
  baith banks till each be won!

Ye'll big wi' me, and I wi' thee,
  ae span, as ow'r the Don;
Lang twyned, we twain, our airch be ane
  though the river o' Time flow on.

(1948)

By Donald Gordon

STRANGE MUSIC

They socht him i' the gloamin',
Fan the shadows fa',
Doon ayont the auld toon brig
Ahin the auld toon wa',
Far the whisperin' croon o' the river
Cam' saft i' the heavy air,
An' the rowans moved sae gently –
Bit naebody wis there.

They socht far the road gaed creepin'
Doon an' ower the haughs,
Atween the whins and heather,
Anaith the siller saughs.
The sough o' the wind i' the branches
Wis the ghaist o' a queer auld sang,
Bit him that they were seekin'
Wis gane frae sicht o' man.

The shepherd tellt o' a laddie
That cam' ower the hill wi' the nicht,
His step wis licht an' free, his e'en
Were fu' o' nae warldly sicht.
He spiert at him fit he wis seekin',
Alane, at close o' day,
Bit 'The music, man, the music!'
Wis a' that he wid say.

I' the grey toon set i' the valley
Seven lang years gaed by.
The water aye lauched anaith the brig
The peat-reek twined tae the sky.
An' anely the saughs by the river
Ever whispered his name:
Bit the wid wis still that mornin'
Fan the wanderer cam' hame.

They fun him aside the river
Far the girse wis saft an' lang,
An' droppin' still i' the wind there cam'
The notes o' a queer, wild sang.
Bit afore they cud catch the lilt o' it
The early cock hid crawn,
An' anely the hidden mavis sang
I' the quaet o' the dawn.

(1939)

45

SANG FOR A LOST LOVER

Nae mair o this, my luve,
Nae mair wi me.
Saft tho yir kiss, my luve,
It canna be.

Ower late wi twa hae met
And nane can end it.
Dear tho I lo'e ye, yet
Kinder tae end it.

The dawn has come, my luve,
Gurly and gray,
The sang is sung, my luve,
Noo ye maun gae.

Yet when ye lie yir lane
Think files on me:
For till I'm auld and dane
I'll mind on thee.

(1983)

By David Gourlay

AULD JEAMES
A SONG

Ye wid think he gat scowth fae his sixty-odd year,
As he woos me wi' ousen and hard-githered gear,
His fine gimmers, his tups, his staigs and his caur,[1]
An' a hoose wi' het water! – I'd seek wide and dae waur!
Yes! an' be his pet yeow for his Cairnton lambs!
Na, na, Jeames! Sough yer sang tae the Mannies o' Glamis,[2]
    The auld stane mannies, the cauld stane mannies,
    The auld and the cauld stane Mannies o' Glamis.

Noo I'll grant he's respeckit at smiddy an' toon,
Wi' a boo for the Laird and puir fowkies a froon,
And on Sabbaths Jeames handles the ladle wi' craft,
Stappin' doon like a Judge fae his seat in the laft.
While the birds piped withoot he'ld hing lang on the Psalms –
For ma kirkin' far better a Mannie o' Glamis,
    An auld stane mannie, a cauld stane mannie,
    An auld and a cauld stane Mannie o' Glamis.

Like a spent sneeshin'-mull he skauls[3] mair than he kens;
Baith his praise an' his priggin's a queyne apprehen's.
When I yoke on him sair till he rins heelster-heels,
Does the gowk ne'er jalouse what a lassikin feels,
That she sighs for het bluid to banish her dwalms
As she picters a mate like a Mannie o' Glamis,
    An auld stane mannie, a cauld stane mannie,
    An auld and a cauld stane Mannie o' Glamis?

If it'd only been Andra – but he lies in France –
The first at the yokin', the last fae the dance!
Wi' a hame for ma faither, a littlin' for me,
I'ld ha' stepped like a queen ower ploo-land and lea,
Facin' poortith and eild 'athoot ony qualms,
An' sent Jeames to tryst wi' the Mannies o' Glamis,
    The auld stane mannies, the cauld stane mannies,
    The auld and the cauld stane Mannies o' Glamis.

[1] Angus for *calves*.
[2] On each side of the north gateway of Glamis Castle stands the rude figure of a naked man, cut out of stone. An Angus version of the English 'Tell that to the Marines' is 'Tell that to the Mannies o' Glamis'.
[3] Angus for *spills*.

(1952)

By Cuthbert Graham

FOR DR NAN SHEPHERD
On her eighty-sixth birthday

Seasons return and the Quarry Wood
blesses you with a continual harvest.
Thanking you for so much good
we ponder as the debt's expressed,
what shall be your badge
in the ever-living Wood of Caledon?
Birch with her silver bark agleam,
or the red-berried rowan saining and sheltering
the young saplings? The noble larch
showering down tassels on a scene
of dappled shade?
Or proud veteran of all, the Scots Pine,
solitary in its shaggy splendour,
symbol of the untameable mountain?

(1979)

By Alexander Gray

IN A MUSIC HALL

Tonight, as I sat in the stalls, idly scanning my programme,
Or watching the figures which flashed out what turn was to come next,
Bored by the knock-about clowns and the tuneless comedians,
Suddenly, raising my eyes for no great entertainment,
All the drab stage was transformed to a temple where beauty,
Hesitant, came to the footlights, afraid yet triumphant;
I, in the presence of Youth, could have bowed down and worshipped
Youth, throwing open her arms to a world still unconquered.

Never again may I see her.   We salute and pass onward,
Receiving and giving, becoming thereafter a memory, –
Often indeed, bestowing a one-sided blessing;
For she whom tonight I silently hailed as the spirit
Of grace and of beauty, of hope and of youthful ambition,
Knows not my name nor aught that makes up my existence.
Yet do I greet her as one who has made my life richer;
Where'er she may go, may God in His goodness be with her.

I should not mind growing old, if we went down together
With all we had loved, linked in a common adventure,
Leaving a darkened world with no beauty to grieve for;
But though the body grows old, the heart remains eager,
Stubborn to find where it will its appointed companions;
And to see strength, being weak; to see youth, being aged;
To witness the promise, and yet be denied the fulfilment, –
O who would die when the rosebuds are still on the hedges?

On the night when I die they will foolishly darken the windows,
And those who have loved me will whisper, as though in the presence
Of one who sleeps lightly, turning and glancing towards me,
There where I lie in the silence that crowns our endeavour.
But, though I pass, in their time all the trees will be joyful,
And without, in the streets, will be beauty and movement and laughter,
And hope and ambition, and love that is mingled in all things.
Old men may die, but youth will continue forever.

And, it may be, on that night, in a far distant city,
Where the lights gleam in the streets which the traffic has polished,
Then in some theatre, rustling, yet hushed and expectant,
When the curtain is raised, a girl may advance to the footlights,
There, for the first time, fronting the crowd and the critic,
Fearful, yet glad; and feeling the power of her beauty,
She will open her arms to the world in a wild exultation; –
If I could, I would cry from my silence: 'May gladness go with you.'

(1928)

By John Gray

A PARAPHRASE
'Go to the ant, thou sluggard . . .', Proverbs vi. 6 ff.

Man, neebor Jock, ye're unco sweir –
Though gleg aneuch at board and beer –
At Martinmas, I 'gin to fear,
Ye'll be escheat and roupit.
It's little wonder that ye're broke,
Ower sune to lowse, ower late to yoke,
Ower mony rypin' the a'e poke,
Ower aft the dram ye've coupit!

Here, tak' a keek aneith this stane,
An' mark the emmets' thrifty train;
The fruits o' hairst they win an' hain
By eident darg diurnal.
They're naggit by nae anxious grieve,
To harass, hound, to drive and deave,
Yet aye gin winter snell achieve
A routhie, plenished girnel.

Wad ye but rise wi' mornin' lark
And kep the tid o' season's wark,
The wolves o' Poortith 'd never bark,
Foul fa' their rabid fever!
But hurcheon-like i' blankets' howe
Ye blink a lazy e'e and rowe,
While a' unmarked abune your pow
Stands Ruin stark the Riever.

(1954)

50

By Gavin Greig

SONG

Far owre Benachie the reed skies o' the evnin'
Hae blawn like a rose and are fadin' awa'
The bonnie hairst moon thro' the branches is sheenin'
The heron's come hame and the far-traivelled craw.

Oh! blest be the hour that renews the heart fever
Yet aids us sae kindly to indulge the dear flame
That sends us awa to the tryst by the river
Yet screens the shy step frae the auld folks at hame.

Sae I'll aff thro' the stooks and alang by the plantin'
For Jamie, dear laddie, is waitin' for me
Where waters are croonin' and moonbeams are slantin'
On yon bonnie simmer-hoose under the tree.

(1995)

By H J C Grierson

LOVE'S HOUR
(From the Dutch of P C Boutens: *Liefdes Uur.*)

'What hour o' the day may it be?'
The pale dawn opens like a rose;
The breast-deep meadow where no mower yet mows
Stand yellow and white with hanging flowers dew-weighted;
The silver stream, a clean-swept highway, flows
Far to the horizon's milky blue;
And morning's singing heart, the sky-lark, throws,
From throat intoxicated,
Wise words wherewith the heart unwitting glows,
Joy that no measure knows,
Joy that seems ever new . . .
'What hour o' the day may it be?'
Love's hour for thee and me!

'What hour o' the day may it be?'
The sun draws nigh the summit of his stair;
And in an ocean of light-saturate air
The cornfield smoulders under glowing gold;
The sickle glitters in the dry, ripe grain;
The shadow shrinks into the wood's dark hold
O'er water-course or in the sky
No cloud goes by;
Only the moon's transparency
Moves ghost-like in the blue unpastured wold . . .
'What hour o' the day may it be?'
Love's hour for thee and me.

'What hour o' the day may it be?'
'Tis Evening; in her russet gold
Grows fair and old
The world's day-lit gaudy face;
A shower of light falls from the heavens apace;
The voices of the winds awake again;
The last wain staggers to the old barn door;
Grey headstones glimmer on the darkling moor;
Above the shining wall
Of the western dunes, in the green of heaven's plain,
Suddenly the Evening star lets fall
Her rays tender and pure . . .
'What hour o' the day may it be?'
Love's hour for thee and me.

(1925)

By Thomas Hardy

THE YOUTH WHO CARRIED A LIGHT

I saw him pass as the new day dawned,
　Murmuring some musical phrase,
Horses were drinking and floundering in the pond,
　And the tired stars thinned their gaze;
Yet these were not the spectacles at all that he conned,
　But an inner one, giving out rays.

Such was the thing in his eye, walking there,
　The real and visible thing,
A close light, displacing the grey of the morning air,
　And the tokens that the dark was taking wing;
And was it not the radiance of a purpose rare
　That might ripe to its accomplishing?

What became of that light? I wonder still its fate!
　Was it quenched at its very apogee?
Did it struggle frail and frailer to a beam emaciate?
　Did it thrive till matured in verity?
Or did it travel on to be a new young dreamer's freight,
　And thence on infinitely?

(1916)

ABERDEEN (April 1905)
'And wisdom and knowledge shall be the stability of thy times.'
　　　　　　　　　　　　　　　　　　　　Isaiah xxxiii. 6.

I looked; and thought, 'She is too gray and cold
To wake the warm enthusiasms of old!'
Till a voice passed: 'Behind that granite mien
Lurks the imposing beauty of a Queen.'
I looked anew; and saw the radiant form
Of Her who stays in stress, who guides in storm;
On the grave influence of whose eyes sublime
Men count for the stability of the time.

(1928)

By Harry R Harries

ECHOES AT KING'S

There broods a quietness at King's at early morning,
As centuries watch each day's insistent dawning,
When summer's sunshine warms the weathered stone,
Or winter's wild wind seeks right to the bone,
Until, with lively fast increasing sound,
The mingling paths with student life abound.

The clearly sounded measured walk,
The sudden hurried scuffle;
The echoing counterpoint of talk;
The secret gravel shuffle.
Footsteps coming, footsteps going,
Fading, distant, into time.

The wheeling gulls with strident cry,
The traffic's rush on cobbles old,
A blackbird scolding somewhere nigh.
Handbells ringing, hourly tolled,
And footsteps coming, footsteps going,
Fading, distant, into time.

(1979)

By J Harrower

FROM THE GREEK ANTHOLOGY

Αἰεί μοι δινεῖ μὲν ἐν οὔασιν ἦχος Ἔρωτος,
  ὄμμα δὲ σῖγα Πόθοις τὸ γλυκὺ δάκρυ φέρει
οὐδ᾽ ἡ νύξ, οὐ φέγγος ἐκοίμισεν, ἀλλ᾽ ὑπὸ φίλτρων
  ἤδη που κραδίᾳ γνωστὸς ἔνεστι τύπος.
ὦ πτανοί, μὴ καί ποτ᾽ ἐφίπτασθαι μέν, Ἔρωτες,
  οἴδατ᾽, ἀποπτῆναι δ᾽ οὐδ᾽ ὅσον ἰσχύετε.

MELEAGER

Whirling ever in my brain
Is a music, Love's refrain,
And my yearning eyes are dim,
With sweet and silent tears abrim.
Night nor day can bring me rest,
On my heart is deep imprest
That familiar character,
Graven of the Sorcerer.
Love imps his wings to fly to me,
His pinions droop when he would flee.

(1922)

By G Rowntree Harvey

THE DREAM AND THE DEED – TRIBUTE TO WILLIAM ELPHINSTONE (extract)

Outside the Chapel of St Mary's College (subsequently King's College), Old Aberdeen, on a May day in the year 1506. Bishop Elphinstone, Principal Hector Boice, and Master of Ceremonies John Molison are grouped together with a retinue of clergy and members of the staff of the University, students and choir singers. Elphinstone speaks:

I love this place, all seasons of the year:
Men of the south who do not know its charm
Think of our northern Aberdeen as only
A tent of skies that has its differing shades
Of grey; as a haunt of snow and rain, of winds
As snell – little they know, who do not live
Upon our seven hills and taste the changing sweets
Of every season here. No other place
I've seen sees autumn come with richer gold,
With lovelier tapestries at dawn or set
Of sun. Often it seems to me our autumn
Is but the birth of spring; thoughts of decay
Can never flourish in this seaward place.
The leaves may fall, the fields be bare, but then
The Don, the Dee grow stronger, swiftlier flow
To meet the sea that has no fading time.

(1931)

BENNACHIE

Sphinx of the Garioch, swart low-couchant ben,
    Gazing on you, the dreams within me rise;
    The long dim corridor of centuries
I tread, and look on days and deeds and men
Forgotten or enshrined by tongue and pen:
    But suppliant thus upon your knees, mine eyes
    Seek ever those vague ancestral memories,
The clouded host who strive through me again
To live, to think, to do, fighting with might
    Against my will and freedom, so my brain
    Rings with the din of war, as once the plain
    Of green Harlaw. . . . O purple Bennachie,
    Dead raiders stained you then, now pity me,
And crown your brows with my pale host this night. . . .

(1926)

By Dorothy E Henderson

BUS JOURNEY HOME

Home travelling home, like a pigeon to dove-cot
Sniffing the keen breeze that wafts from the sea,
Breath-taking glimpse of the fay town of Gourdon,
Harbour and rocks, frothing waves running free.
On we go on past soft sweep of pale harvest field,
Yellow and shining, the stubble blades gleam
Caught by the sunlight, left by the garnered yield,
Proud and accomplished, with satin-smooth sheen.
Dunnottar, its noble walls huddled, lies dreaming,
Bungalows, cottages, cattle sweep by,
Barley fields waiting the harvester's gleaning
Stretch in their glory, and climb to the sky.

Potato fields, shaw-burnt, wait for the lifting,
Mayweed and mustard with poppies glow bright.
There hovers a kestrel, with pointed wings quivering,
Expectantly poised, then hid from my sight.
But home, I am home, with the rapture still clinging,
Crossing again our dear River Dee,
Back to the heart of the grey Granite City,
Sparkle of sunshine on house, spire and tree,
Plaint of the herring gull, circling the trawler fleet,
Cold salt tang of our Aberdeen sea.

(1977)

By Hamish Henderson

LAMENT FOR THE SON
(Translated from Corrado Govoni)

He was the most beautiful son on earth,
braver than a hero of antiquity,
gentler than an angel of God:
tall and dark, his hair like a forest,
or like that intoxicating canopy
which spreads over the Po valley;
and you, without pity for me, killed him
– there, in a cave of dull-red sandstone.

He was the whole treasure
of war, of sanctuary and of crown,
of my accepted human poverty,
of my discounted poetry –
You, once his hiding-place was discovered
(after which no angel could sleep) –
You, with your thieving hands
that were strangers to no sacrilege,
you carried him away at the run
into the darkness
to destroy him without being seen –
before I had time to cry out:
'Stop!
'Put him down!
'*That is my son!*'

He was my new sun, he was the triumph
of my betrayed boyhood;
and you changed him, in front of my praying hands
into a heap of worms and ashes.
    Mutilated, hurt, blinded,
only I know the tragic weight I am carrying.
I am the living cross of my dead son.

And that tremendous and precious weight
of such great suffering, of such unbearable glory
becomes daily harder and more heavy;
it breaks my skin,
it fractures every joint,

it tears my soul:
and yet I shall have to carry it
as my sole good –
as long as I have one beat
of love in my old veins for him.
I shall carry him, sinking on to my knees, if I have to,
until the day of my own burial.
Only then will we be down there together,
a perfect and obscure cross.

['Lament for the Son' is part of a long prose poem, here re-cast in verse, written by Govoni after the death of his son Aladino, a partisan of Italy, who was one of 335 hostages shot by the S.S. under Kappler in the Ardeatine Caves, 24 March 1944.]

(1987)

By Irene Hughson

DAFFODILS

I put some daffodils in a vase,
And now I have
Six suns glowing in one room,
With a delicateness
The sun has not.
They make a Springtime
Out of a cold, bleak day.
Their yellowness
Eclipses quite
The weak rays from the window
Where a cubist huddle
Of grey slate lies framed.

They open themselves to me,
Their petals thrown wide
In an ecstasy of beginning,
But knowingly they keep
Their deep hearts secret and untouchable.

(1967)

By May C Jenkins

THE EXILE

A river rins frae heath'ry hills,
  Ower whitenin' stanes, to reach the sea;
I played aboot its banks, an' thocht
  Nae sicht wad be sae dear to me.

A river rins frae heath'ry hills,
  By girss sae green! – In aul' distress
I socht its croonin', soothin' sang;
    Its peace wad ease ma weariness.

A river rins frae heath'ry hills.
  Beneath the trees. O, micht I ken –
Instead o' dust an' dryin' heat –
  That siller gramarye again!

(1960)

ROADS IN RAIN

We walk the rain-dulled roads
of Aberdeen;
our anger darkens love.

Milk-bottles clink
on steps;
doors open, shut.

People go hunched in the rain,
rushing last walks
with their dogs.

An occasional car leaps out
like a vast greyhound
from a side street.

'Why should we quarrel?'
you say,
taking my hand.

And grief is gone,
discarded in the streets;
a quiet comes.

Your touch is feather-soft –
but granite-strong –
dismissing rain.

(1967)

61

By D A Kidd

TO POSTUMUS
(*Horace Odes* 11, 14)

Ah, Postumus, the years fly on apace,
And virtue will not save the ageing face
From timely wrinkles, or defer the day
When Death shall overtake thee in the race.

And think not, Postumus, thou canst allay
With thrice an hundred hecatombs a day
Grim Pluto, who reduced the giants twain,
Geryon and Tityus, to own his sway.

For all who eat the fruits of earth must make
That final passage of the nether lake,
Though some, on passing, wealth and fame forgo,
And some the paths of penury forsake.

In vain, secure from bloody war we thrive,
And the loud billows of the sea survive;
In vain we shun the pestilential airs
Of baleful Autumn and escape alive:

Before us yet the murky waters loom
Of slow Cocytus on beyond the tomb,
Where the dishonoured Danaids await,
And Sisyphus who serves his endless doom.

With home and lands thy loving consort fades,
Nor any tree of all thy garden glades
Save the accursed cypress in the end
Shall bear its mortal master to the shades.

A worthier heir shall drink the vintage hoard
That thou hast safely in thy cellar stored,
And spill with insolence upon the ground
Far richer drops than grace a princely board.

(1946)

By Douglas Kynoch

NINE GWEED RIZZENS

Melpomene was mumpin;
And her een were rubbit reid;
She lookit unco dowie,
As gin somebody was deid.

Terpsichore was trachelt;
But, for a' she had tae pech,
Was loupin like a limmer
Wi a forkie or a flech.

Thalia, she was scraichin
Like a half-dementit hen;
Fut set the lassie lauchin
Only her and Clootie ken.

Thon Erato had likely
Fuspert something till 'er. Och,
An affa deem for fusprins.
Ay, and aye that bittie roch.

Urania was scuttrin
Wi some ferlie in the skies;
And Clio was teen up wi
A historical treatise.

Euterpe was forfochen
Aifter feeplin at her flute;
Polymnia was ailin;
And Calliope was oot.

Mount Helicon was heelster-
Gowdie a' damt aifterneen;
And that's the wye I never
Got my magnum opus deen!

(1983)

A YOUNG CHIEL
(A translation of *Un Jeune Homme* by André Chénier)

Fan I was but a bairn, this big and bonnie quine
Wad gie's a smile and ca me owre aside her syne.
And, stannin on her lap, my loonie's han was eesed
Tae rinnin throwe her hair; and owre her face and briest.
And whiles, yon han o hers that straikit me sae croose
Made on as though tae flyte bairn cantrips nae that douce.
Twas aye afore her lads, dumfoonert at it aa,
The prood and sonsie jaud wad dawt on's maist ava.
The times my face has felt the smoorichs o her moo!
(Though, michty, neen o't meant fat it wad mean till's noo!)
And aye the herds wad say, fan seein they were beat:
'It's wicket wastrie 'at! Yon bairn's a lucky breet!'

(1986)

By W Gordon Lawrence

MIDDLE AGE LOVE
(after Tagore)

You remain silently in my heart
filling my middle years
with a perfume like that
of Rajanigandha,
Queen of the Night.

My soul once lost in
the inane profanities
of the technologies
of knowing
is now suffused
subtly as sandalwood,
with expectations of revelation.

One revelation through loving
is of the sacredness
of giving while living;
otherwise death will be joining
the host of lost opportunities.

(1986)

EXILES

Some of us were born for Exile:
cleared for sheep; or
herds for dogs of war;
refugees from revolution;
programmed for extermination.

But some of us have Exile chosen,
to be outwith those Pale paradigms
of others who are cradled in
shawled shells of comfort certain.

Life becomes in
seas of chaos,
typhoons of doubts,
nonces of noughts.

Mind holes in blind space are ours of choice,
questing neoteric echoes of our voice.

(1979)

By John B Logan

WEE JOHNNIE FROST

Wee Johnnie Frost cam' aroun' yestere'en,
An' cantrip'd an' capered withoot bein' seen;
An' mony's the body that kent tae their cost,
That they'd had a veesit frae wee Johnnie Frost.

He danced doon the street on a cauld blast o' win',
Lik' a wee wisp o' sillar blawn doon frae the mune.
An' aye as he capered ilk stick, stane, an' post
Was dustit wi' starlicht by wee Johnnie Frost.

He cam' tae the brig, an' peered doon at the burn,
An' the watter a' clotted lik' milk in a churn,
An' quated its owercome as sune as he crost,
Fair scunner'd an' chitterin', wi' wee Johnnie Frost.

He loupit the dyke, an' cam' intae the yaird,
An' poked wi' lang fing'rs as laigh as he dared:
The hale o' the neeps an' the tatties were lost,
Ower the heid o' the cantrips o' wee Johnnie Frost.

He keeked thro' the windy, blae neb at the pane,
An' lauched tae himself lik' a hullicate wean;
Then a' thro' the hoose, lik' a flichterin' ghost,
Stappin' heigh on his tiptaes, went wee Johnnie Frost.

He went to the folk that were courriein' in bed,
An' pinched them wi' fing'rs as cauld as the lead;
There were rowth o' puir bodies that rose wi' a hoast,
An' pit a' the blame upo' wee Johnnie Frost.

Afar ower the muir cam' the gray licht o' dawn,
An' the cock gied a screitch frae a yaird near at haun';
He glow'red roun' aboot him as if he were lost,
Then aff lik' a whitterick gaed wee Johnnie Frost.

(1925)

GLORY DEPARTED

They do not wear the toga now:
the old familiar scarlet gown
no more in King's Quadrangle flares
and stars the grey streets of the Town.

No more within the chapel walls
about the holy bishop's tomb
deep ranks of upturned faces shine
over a scarlet-tinctured gloom.

No more upon the benches tall
tier upon tier tumultuously
conning Greek verses, bajans sit
girt in their glorious panoply.

No more about the gates of King's
and up and down her quiet ways
the red blood ebbs and flows; no more
those strong heart-beats of former days.

Only a girl walks, there, and there,
clad in this so conspicuous red,
slow in her tarrying gait, like some
late blood-drop creeping from the dead.

The flaming leaves have left the tree,
the red autumnal sun gone down;
only a dead, dead winter reigns
within the College and the Town.

(1975)

By J M Lothian

I WILL WALK PROUDLY ON ST ANDREW'S DAY

Grey Island that I love, and greystone homesteads,
Brown hills, and craggy shore, and wheeling mew,
Bare, wind-swept, sleepy towns with cobbled causeways,
I will walk proudly when I think of you.

Proudly I'll walk, for now my heart remembers
Names set like gems, of martyr, hero, bard,
Forgers of freedom who fought Roman and the Saxon,
Haters of tyranny: Fate made your way most hard.

Dear lovely land of memory and of dreaming,
Through Time made timeless, and through Thought made free,
Your name is set like rock mid moving waters
Proud am I walking as I think of thee!

(1951)

By M S Lumsden

THE CHACKIE-MULL I THE WUD

Wheesht! Hearken! D'ye hear him there, ahin yer heid,
Tick, tick, tickin i the wa,
The eerie chackie-mull tick, tickin i the wud?
I'm feart deith's nae far awa.

Losh! Ye're easy fleyt, like a muckle gockit nowt;
Yon's nae deith but life.
There's nocht but a sma broon golachy there
Chap, chap, chappin tull his wife.

(1959)

By Alastair Macdonald

VAUX-LE-VICOMTE

High-hatted, erect on seat of water,
she fronts you with dowager hauteur,
no more than a shade wan
from centuries' homage to her spell. And then
on south façade the gold smile of the bow,
radiant to far point of vista-ed geometry.
Inviolate still, who in her youth
saw best of the Grand Siècle:
Lully, Molière – all that.

Today, a July morning, two or three
wander the sun-dried emptiness: girls jeaned,
a woodsman puttering distance on a bike.
Where long transverse canal dies through
to mud pool in the trees, boys fish,
as forebears did from those razed villages.

But not to slight
a splendour as of too high cost.
Now, the creation lures, because apart,
in grandeur and planned peace,
asserting what, with luck, a mortal caught
in way of paradise.
Dream of a doomed Icarus, but made
by genius, and in time to stay,
a tribute to that taste.

Let them not pass to vandals, and the sheep
Of Philip Larkin's churches: Blenheim,
Chatsworth, when His Grace no longer can.

Prized out of pigeon-holes and cares,
here we may yet touch space,
in scent of box and water breathe the years.

(1986)

70

By A C Mackenzie

CONTRA MUNDUM

Beyond the velvet curtains of the grave,
  Beyond the silence of its desolate hall,
I see them stand whose eyes no boast can brave,
  Whose hearts no lie enthrall.

Whether we enter in with loud fanfare,
  Or to our judges creep with sighing sound,
We cannot tell what wreaths will wither there,
  What lowly heads be crowned.

(1940)

By Agnes Mure Mackenzie

ARTEMISIA
returning from the country in a London fog, receives a gift of flowers.

> In city staleness, where the day is night,
> My time of sweet clean light and fragrance closes:
> When suddenly, the fragrance and the light
> Are in my hands again, caught in your roses.

(1925)

SILVIUS TO PHOEBE

> I may succeed: more likely I shall fail.
> You'd rest indifferent though I had done well.
> But my disaster's naught that you'd bewail:
> I carry that much comfort into hell.

(1926)

By Colin A McLaren

DOCUMENTS 1746–1790
(displayed in a Bicentennial exhibition)

I Proclamation, 1746
Vanquished, we bled in caves and turned our faces westward.
Destitute, we clawed up roots and gorged until we sickened.
Proscribed, we sang laments and sailed for Carolina.
Victims, comments Glasgow, of an obsolete feudality.
In clanship our security.

II Letters home, 1750
. . . 'tis a Countrey very good for a Puir Man . . .
Frugality is much esteem'd. No Father will disparage
The Thrifty Scot who, ill-endowed, Advancement seeks by Marriage.
And if, once wedded, he should prove both Sober and Industrious.
. . . all White People are upon a Common Footing . . .
Equality assured! No Creed but freely tolerated.
Nor Rank, Estate nor Force-of-Arms but *Virtue* venerated.
No honest Zeal, no zealous Toil but faithfully rewarded.
Companionship to every man but lately come accorded.
. . . save Dutch and other Foreigners that are not much regarded.

III Map of a plantation, 1763
. . . Oakland . . .
Black Jack, Harp Leaf, Hairy Leaf, Water White,
Chinquapin and Sandy Red, Downy Red and Scarlet –
Arthritic peers, ill-named for an arboreal elite,
Unmindful of the hogs that snuffle acorns at their feet.
. . . Swamp . . .
Its density oppresses us.
A shred-hung, splintered bone is hefted in resentment
And in defiance thrown.
Awakes a sleeper.
Looses time.
A saurian snout steers vengefully towards us
Through the slime.
. . . Sandy soil . . .
Salt and nitre, fortifying, guarantee its worth;
One needs but to turn the superficies of earth.
An agronomist's sanguine prediction
We prove beyond doubt to be
Fictitious.

IV Inventory of property, 1772
Syphax, carpenter.
Nero, Waggoner.
London and Tiberius, prime field slaves.
Tinkery, ruptured.
Rachel, runaway.
Moody, an idiot mute.
He crouches, catching at the echoes of the talking drum,
The low, enticing flute.

V Claim for compensation, 1786
We took no side
But planted rice, popilions and indigo.
They, questioning our loyalty,
Sent threats of confiscation.

We took no side
But cropped our rice, popilions and indigo.
They offered terms: their lenity,
Our oath of abjuration.
We took no oath.
They seized our rice, popilions and indigo
And in the name of Liberty
. . . For men were mad for Liberty . . .
They ravaged the plantation.

VI Epitaph, 1790
Banished by rebels, who were banished for rebellion;
Penalized by Loyalists, who would not swear allegiance;
Abased, we begged for recompense, who scorned to beg a pardon.
Victims, comments Oxford, of Life's exquisite irony.
We died in squalid penury.

(1977)

By Anne MacLeod

ICARUS

The cloud sea drifts into the morning sky.
Under your wing I linger, would remain
safe in the aqua fading into blue.
Soft clouds below obscure the sodden earth
the mountain's dark insistence, and the sprawl
of cities forced into the light of day
out of the night's warm slumber.
                                    Here with you
curled in your arms, love-drowsed, I do not hear
the break of day, the passing of our dawn.
the morning's dappled call. I can ignore
the sun that plays upon your golden wings,
warm now and soft; too late I wake and turn
shocked by the sudden heat, the burning wax –
surely we will not fall?

                                                (1990)

ORAN MOR

There are songs, and there is oran mor,
piobaireachd of the human chanter –
who will sing if these notes fail?
Who can bind the wind?

Reeds bend before the storm, flowers
fade upon the machair, seeds
driven by the bean-shith fervour of the gale
into droning hibernation

at the island's edge. The sun shall
rise again, but to what new music? The seed
may fall on lazy-beds of bitter generation,
or germinate
in bleak despair on the bare shingle,
one step from extinction.

                                                (1990)

By Isobel M Mearns

ORCHESTRA

Preliminary tinkering – scraping.
Tuning in fifths – reminiscence of the 'Danse Macabre'.
The baton raised – pause.
A hush – a hush of tongues of the onlookers,
A holding of breath – expectancy – concentration –
To miss the beat, to be out when the baton falls –
To have mistuned a string, to pluck or to touch prematurely
With nervous fingers.
Silence.

But no. Fence taken.
The shrill of the violins, the boom of the bass,
The call of the horn, the complaining mellowness
Of the 'cello, the other-worldly caress
Of the flute, the patter of the drum,
The swell, the boom, the crash.
The crescendo of melody. And suddenly
The orchestra is not a conglomeration
Of individual instruments held and played
At intervals, by individual people,
But an entity, a being, and a force
Where separateness is lost, or rather merged,
Merged on a plane of power. And so the player,
Second fiddle perhaps, in the third back row,
Pours forth enchantment that never fills his room
When he toilfully fingers his instrument, thinking of technique,
Melody also, of course – but that difficult passage!
Twice the speed that *he* can manage with ease. . . .
The conductor – what did he say of the other fellow?
He'd get what you missed? Yes – of course – and then safety,
The safety of numbers.

This is no safety, but being.
There are no players, conductor or baton or score
Impinging separately, no gazing audience,
No difficult passages – only orchestra –
Orchestra – orchestra.
Each is caught up in a whirl of concerted feeling,
Each plays as he has not played, nor shall play again
Till orchestra reclaims him – that strange force.
Tentativeness is gone, and in its place
Comes power.

The audience trickles forth, the lights go out,
Slowly – but out.
The players emerge into the dripping streets
In twos and threes, with instruments under their arms –
Individuals, with instruments.
Melody gone, and only noise in the streets,
Yet that alone does not mark irretrievable loss.
A tram clangs – 'bus brakes screech.
Orchestra has fled.
In the dimness one lamp sways –
One lamp – swings – sways.

(1939)

By Royston J Milne

THE STEEN SODGER

Gin it's caul' an' dreich an' dowie; gin it's sattlet kin' or fair
There's a lad ye'll aye see standin' a' his lee-lane i' the Square
Heich abeen th' argy-bargy on a muckle granite steen
Wi's rifle in's ae hand and a hand that shades his een.

Come the mornin' sun, new-yokit; come the meen, an' fyles a star,
Yon lad ne'er divals fae listenin' tae the winds that traivel far;
And there's nae a byre-door steekit, nor there's niver a leaf stirred
Nor a coble's tether streekit that the sodger hisna heard.

Fan the lift's a' mirkit ower an' the meen's sair hauden doon,
Fan the bonny gowden windows blink their een ower a' the toon,
Fan a win's fuffin' an' soughin' ower the ley an' throu' the breers,
Gin ye speir at the steen sodger then, he'll tell ye a' he hears.

'Heich or laich, the souns I hear are a' the souns I kent afore
(Bar the putter o' a tractor faur the horseman learnt his lore)
And the caller winds come souffin' wi' a sang frae ilka airt;
Fyles the cankle o' a kirk-bell, fyles the vrattle o' a cairt,
Or a wheeshin' whirrication faur the pertrick echt her nest.
Fyles the feeplin' o' wee quinies as they warsle throu' a test,
Syne a muckle salmon loupin' in a pool abeen Blairdaff,
(Aye, an' syne a poacher pechin' as he raxes wi' the gaff).
Hine awa, the screich o' timmer faur the sawyer's slabbin' logs;
Fae the commonty, the yelpin' o' a tinker body's dogs;
While a turn o' "Tullochgorum", fustled saftly doon the fleed,
Marks a chiel that hopes anither hairst'll connach his Trust Deed.
Fae the stytin' o' the baker's dosened early mornin' beets
An' the auld wife's Monday mangle (wi' the weety clap o' sheets)
Tae the gweedman's forenicht fiddle as he gars his elbuck jeuk
An' laich lauchin' i' the gloamin' fae a weel-remembered neuk –
Man, they're nae that muckle different fae the soun's I left ahin'
An' they're bonny, bonny, bonny, are the wylin's o' the win.'

(1958)

By Virginia Scott Miner

ROOTS

The leaf-years drop away, when greenness clothed
my world. Now upper branches creak in storm,
break off and fall. But roots remain –
all that is left of hope – resisting still
the buffeting of years.
       Only the consciousness
of those deep roots, solid in earth
consoles as dry leaves drift – for from a root,
who knows what yet may rise?

The strength of life lies in the roots. All else is decoration,
and though three hundred years have passed
since my own forebears left their lochs and glens
it is as if I'd been there half my life, had always known
how skirling pipes assail the skies,
crying defiance while admitting grief.

Now I must hear them on their native ground,
must see belled heather on the hills,
must watch the golden gorse light up the land, see shadows tell
their timeless time.
   I must go home to Scotland once again.

               (1975)

By J Leslie Mitchell (Lewis Grassic Gibbon)

TO MARGUERITE ('PEGGY')

The streets are very wet, the War-God weeps
Over the harvest that the whirlwind reaps.
(My metaphor is mixed, but what of that?)
The sense is there, rhyme is neat and pat).
I stand beneath a lamp whose sickly light
Fitfully gleams through the silent night
And casts weird shadows on the houses near
While Union Street lies shimmering, gaunt and sere,
And good folks, all behind the barréd door
Until the dawn comes, lie sleeplessly – or snore.
But what care I – far in the Western night
A patch of stars, frost-tinged, is golden bright,
The moon, of whom the Easterns once did rave
Is wanly white (The times have made her grave);
And so I'll sing a song of Marguerite,
She who is lovely, smiling-eyed and sweet.

One thing I hate – and faith! I never can –
Jot down a girl's points one by one.
Yet most I love to see your tender gaze
Like a sunlit moor in summer haze,
For in your eyes are things that do not cease,
Wistfulness, joy and a quiet touch of peace:
Like to shadows, that, as daylight goes,
The sun casts where the silent streamlet flows
Or as the new moon o'er the fields of May
Changing unchangeless, though scarce born a day.

I mind me well of a far-distant age
When alligator steak was all the rage
When older folk oft met a sudden fate
Between the jaws of progeny ungrate
And beds of hemlock laid within a cave
Couches for dreams of happy lovers gave
How, just one beauteous moonlit night like this
I tasted the first glories of your kiss.
The air was hot and moist as is the way
Of swampy southern lands e'en to this day
The brooding woods on either side were quiet
Yet full of life and Passion's joyous riot
And when, with whispers soft and shining eyes
We drank that stream, Ye Gods! 'twas Paradise.

But time has passed while I have had my say,
Those streaks above the roofs bring in the day
And three o'clock the Town House bell now states
Has brought the morn banging at our gates.
And I've been dreaming till my head is sore,
Peggy! – But that's a name that I abhor! –
Marguerite of roses! (Speak of Satan's fall!)
What, by the way, are you to me at all?
You smile, I raise my hat when e'er we meet
What, I ask you, Oh ye powers above,
In all the Universe can compare with – Love!
Who brings the sage from out his solitude
And leaves the saint in an unsaintly mood,
Who makes such fools as I at this late hour
Stand and declaim the glories of his power
– Ah, Marguerite, wert thou here not thus 'twould be
But in some silent nook where none might see,
Your hand in mind (tight-squeezed) to make me bold
To whisper things that prudery leaves untold:
And see the lights within your star-like eyes
Gleam like the shimmering sheens of Paradise
To watch a careless tendril of your hair
Caressed across your cheek by the still air
And see your lips with just that lingering smile
Banish the dusk and dimness, all the while
I – but what's the use? Alas, you are not here;
(Talking has made me dry –
Oh for a jug of beer!)

And all I've said is 'bosh' that's hard to beat;
But oh! I wish that I were once again
Back in the caves where lived the first of men,
Or sat once more within the forest dread
Waiting for you to come by love-signs led
Out of the gloom and through the still moonlight!
For there would be no need to say 'Good Night!'

(1989)

81

By Mary Montgomery

CHA MHÒR

Nuair a bha mi beag
Cha mhòr
Nach do chaill mi a' Ghàidhlig
Mar a chaill mi a rabaid dhubh
A thachd air curran
Agus na sgilleanan
Agus na peansailean
Agus na griogagan bréagh' air lastaig
A bhris mi nuair a bha an siorcas
Ann an Ceann-a-bhàigh

Nam bithinn air a call
'S dòcha gum faodainn bhith nam bhall
De dh'ealt dheas

Yes yes

ALMOST

When I was little
I almost
Lost my Gaelic
Like I lost the black rabbit
That choked on a carrot
And the pennies
And the pencils
And the bonnie beads on elastic
I broke at the circus
In Bayhead

If I had
I could maybe be a member
Of a right-wing flock

Quack quack

(1993)

By Ken Morrice

BUCHAN

There is a rocky shelf of land
That juts its jaw in the sea.
The fields are weathered hard and dour
Like the folk. Scree more than tree
Fills the landscape. East winds
Harness the wavetops and scatter lochs,
Secret, small and nameless,
Beside the rowans and whins, eyes of blue
On the rough, blind face of the moor.
Square cottages cluster cliff-perched
Before the glittering sea,
Where tattered gulls in tiny harbours
Splash their paint on flaking concrete jetties.
Here the people lived under God's stern hand.

Digging stones from barren land,
With characteristic thrift they built them
Into dykes, enclosing like a fold
Their hard-won fertility, their ripening gold,
Labouring a monument
That still rebukes the red frivolity of poppies
In the corn. Where the Bullers roar
Families cast for silver, or near Girdleness
Harvested fish in this north Galilee.
The granite teeth of the hungry coast
Have fathomed deep a cortege from the sea
And stand as massive gravestones
Over skeletons of ships and ghosts of men who cry
'It is appointed unto man to die.'
Fast bound in fiery creeds and faith
(Some preferring lusty sinning)
The fishers built their churches, raised their choirs
To Him who told a kingdom first to fishermen;
And waited the Archangel's trumpet death to time.

This race is dead and gone.
Little boats are big business.
But still the life can be seen, paradoxically,
In graveyards among the cold stone
Angels, doves and fouled anchors,
Beside the pallid flowers that wax
Entombed in domes of glass.
There they lie who fathered me;
And say yet on their tombstones
That rise amid the loud flat silences,

83

'Storms past, safe at last',
Promising, 'Till the morning break',
Confident, 'In that bright glory',
Or arrogantly, 'Be ye also ready'.

(1961)

NIGG

Time alone separates the dull red
Granite of these cliffs and the red
Clay in the kirkyard yonder.
As I stand on this gray day,
With scarce a breath to sunder
The wetness of air and sea,
Let my living and my dead
Surround me. Let them say
Who carried the sea upon his back,
What fish sucked the marrow from whose bones,
Drifting like the untidy sea-wrack,
Whose blood seeps now to colour the clay
Of the ploughed field and the crimson cliff.

I would have written an epitaph
To please them and to honour the good,
The mortal drudgery, the valour
That lies now beneath the cold wet gravestones.
But the whistling peewit mocks my mood.
And anyway they would not have understood.

(1962)

DOMICILIARY VISIT

'Dr Watt spiered at you to call, did he?
Weel, jist you cam awa ben.
My man's no in yet, as you can see.
Fit did you say your name wis again?
A psychiatrist! Michtie me,
I thocht it wis the insurance mannie.

O, you maun forgie my menners.
Sit you doon, I'll pit aff the TV,
and get the money. My man's denner's
still tae mak. But dearie me, I maun be
gaun gyte! You're nae the insurance man,
are you? Fit wey hiv you come tae see me?

I ken I'm wearing aul, but I'm nae saft.
No me! I wis tap o the class for sums
and best in the schule at needle-craft.
Some quines are aathegither thooms,
but I wis aye skeely and the teacher's pet.
Psychiatrist you say? You dinna surely think

I'm daft? I canna mind the date or foo mony
years I was mairrit. The Prime Minister?
That wid be Mister Churchill. Na, na,
that's nae richt either. Is it Mister
Wilson? O laddie, it's nae eese ava.
Since my man deid I dinna read ony

papers, but I watch the telly ilky day.
My favourite programme? I jist canna
mind the noo. I'm ravelled – a bit fey
wi aa yon different peels. But you mauna
take me awa. I'm jist fine, richt here
faur I bide. Onywey, fa wad mak my husband's tea?'

(1992)

85

By Robin Munro

PATTERNS

A thin line of logic holds Aberdeen
from the South, an invisible tripwire
you can break, but only once (like logic),
one hard and complete time.

You are on the ground,
the world's hatred stouning.

'There was a woman stabbit
yestreen in Aberdeen'
our simple man is telling me
'that never used tae happen.'

His line to the past is easy broken
for all the pattern was long in making.
I hear him trying to find a single strand, by day.
I stumble through a night-time of it.

(1975)

SONATA

Mozart's piano; a warm Sunday morning
drifts wider, grows finer,
the lace is of leaves
and several grasses.

The grasses allow you, the leaves
bend to touch you, they feel their way
into your mind – on a Sunday,

you think green, and smell time,
taste the old north moor,
the bodies touching.

They ease together, keys,
and dance.
For human fingers
they join and dance.

(1974)

By Charles Murray

"AIBERDEEN AWA' "
Dedicated – by an Associate Member – to the Aberdeen University
Club of South Africa)

O sair forfochen here wi' heat
I weary for the wind an' weet
An' drivin' drift in Union Street
    Fae th' Duke to Bauby Law.
Then mak' my bed in Aiberdeen
An' tak' me back I'll no compleen
Tho' a' my life I lie my leen
    In Aiberdeen awa'.

I fain would dook in Dee aince mair
An' clatter doon the market stair –
O the caller dulse an' partans there!
    The fish-wives' mutches braw!
Neth Marischal's spire or King's auld croon,
In hodden gray or scarlet goon,
For future fechts we laid the foun'
    In Aiberdeen awa'.

In mony an unco airt I've been,
An' mony a gallant city seen,
Yet here the nicht we'll drink to ane
    Can vaunt it ower them a'.
They say! They say! Fat say they than?
Well, jist e'en lat them say, my man.
While, clean caup oot an' hand in han',
    Here's "Aiberdeen Awa'."

(1913)

87

HORACE I. 9.
Vides ut alta stet nive candidum Soracte

Drift oxter deep haps Benachie,
Aneth its birn graens ilka tree,
The frost boun' burn nae mair is free
    To bicker by.

Haud on the peats an' fleg the cauld,
An' ere the hoast gets siccar hauld
Yon luggit pig o' fower year auld
    Sall first gang dry.

On Providence oor cares we'll cast,
The power that stirs will lay the blast
When larch an' rodden firm an' fast
    Will stand ance mair.

Whatever comes we'll grip the day,
It's oors to drink an' dance an' play,
The morn can bring us what it may –
    Grey heads or sair.

Let gloamin' find us wooers still
True to oor trysts by haugh or hill,
The lassie's lauch will guide you till
    She's catch'd an' kiss't.

Syne thieve her brooch or slip wi' care
The ribbon fae her touzled hair,
Half heartit struggles but declare
    She'll never miss't.

(1914)

FATE FURLS THE TOTUM
RONDEAU

Fate furls the totum. What like chance hae we?
Wha kens the bias? Neither you nor me.
   Ae year or auchty, tho' the rig may rin,
   Fae bairnhead on, we're a' owre keen to win
Ever to heed how fest the forenichts flee.

Set roon the board, we risk wi' eager e'e
Oor wee bit plans an' preens, but fail to see
   Bonnie an' fairly tho' it seems to spin,
       Fate furls the totum.

For ane we tak' fu' seen we dossie three;
What's tint is by, we look for what may be,
   Till nickle-naething shortly droons oor din,
   An' rantit bare as when we first begin
The Grave tak's a'; syne, syne owre late the plea
       Fate furls the totum.

(1927)

By Geoffrey A Oelsner

SONG FOR ABERDEEN

Aberdeen,
I will remember your mothgrey streets,
daubed with yellow daffodils,
the devil in your pubs
playing accordion,
the tall ships
rigged with dreams
in your misty harbour.
Aberdeen,
King's College saturated
with thought,
tier upon tier of leatherbound volumes,
the cobblestone river
shining in noon light
I will remember.
There is a circular hill
above Seaton,
above the humming mills by the Don,
where I heard your song
blow seaward on a soughing gull-wind,
Aberdeen.
It was a song
that welled from the granite,
a darkness heavy and black
as galactic space.
It exploded forth as the green crowns
of trees in Spring,
with undertones of wind
strumming the grass harp.
There were sounds of people:
singing, fighting,
pivoting from pain to sleep
to morning hope.
The woman in the shop
selling pastries,
the school children subverted
by sun and giggles
from Latin,
the bus conductor's
'Both sides now,'
the paperseller shouting
evening's gospel from his corner pulpit
(Amazing Full-Page Picture)
all these interwove
and the chorus blew by,

it passed through the long beach-grasses
and was taken into the roar of the sea.
So it has been
since before Elphinstone,
before St Machar's,
before even the oldest rainbeaten gravemarkers.
Since the first settlers
laid stone upon stone,
lit fire in hearth,
spoke together in a tongue
closer to the wind's syntax
than our own,
the sea,
the deep and heavy darkness,
has taken all your songs.
But you have taken
from her,
made silver from the glistening
scaled silver in the nets,
suffering wind-lash and rope-burn
to do this.
The voices of sailors lost at sea
ring up like vertigo.
I hear faint cries
as your ships plough eastward,
Aberdeen.
They are not from gulls.

Outside the city,
gunmetal grey combers
drive in toward the beach.
It is twilight.
The sun casts that
strange Angelus light
that limns the fence-wires,
barn roofs
infuses the hushed earth.
Looking to your foundries
with their great fists of smoke
clenched above the city,
looking to the cage of lights
blinking on,
I know I will remember you as a home,
Aberdeen.
Remember that first loneliest night,
the parade of friends dancing
through bars, classrooms,
dorm rooms.

Your beer struck a gong in my head
that hasn't stopped ringing.
Smoky conversations, an archive
of faces circle in the memory.
Not the memory, however,
but the moments themselves,
are the value,
beads in a life full of feeling
flashing beyond analysis,
dancing joyously and aware on the razor's edge.
So while I am here
I celebrate,
adding my voice to your sea-bound song,
Aberdeen.

(1971)

By Ian Olson

STRATHCONON

When you took the autumn to London
And left me to burrow into winter
I said they could pack up Strathconon
And box up the birch and the larch;
Return the hawks and the geese
The swans upon Achonachie,
And while they were about it
They could empty the Curin dam.

There was, after all, no point
In the upkeep of Torr Achilty
In preserving the pines of Achlorachan
And sustaining the pass of Scardroy;
No need to retain Inverchoran
For the sake of a handful of eagles
Or maintain the forest of Meinich
For the amusement of the deer.

. . . . . .

Last night when I entered Strathconon
The birches were naked and mourning
The larch trees stripped and shivering
And the pines smothered in sleet;
By Dalbreac the river was silenced
From Craig Ruadh the deer uplifted
The dams preserved in ice
And the mountains blacked out by the snow.

(1985)

By H Philsooph

A MIRAGE IS NOT A MIRAGE

In this great desert
Whose body is half-dead
With thirst and loneliness,
What is called, at a distance, a mirage,
Is the naked mind of the desert,
Which the thought, the faith,
And the love of water
Have filled and made alive.

(1989)

By Douglas S Raitt

THE BLESSIN' O' LEARNIN'
In memory of 'Rab the Rhymer', the author of *Town and Gown*, whose
death occurred on 4 October 1944.

The blessin' o' learnin' (says aul' Tammas Quinn)
Foo it plays up the deil wi' yer kith an' yer kin:
If ye hinna't ye're telt that it's brains that ye need;
Fan ye're gien't it's infernal for gaun till yer heid,
A saxmonth o' College till some fan they're young
An' their stammacks turns ower at their ain mither tongue.
Oh, the Learnin's a blessin', bit tak it fae me,
There's a lot to be learnt besides Learnin'.

A skeirie bit gravat, a buik i' the han',
And a pipe, disna mak ony bra'er a man;
And a sicht seener stick tae the Buchan like me
Than mooth the King's English the wye some fowks dee.
The blessin' o' learnin' o' some maks richt feels,
An' the lassies if onything mair than the chiels.
Oh, the Learnin's a blessin', bit tak it fae me,
There's a lot to be learnt besides Learnin'.

It's astonishing, though, foo the classical Don
Wi' his smattrin' o' Greek and o' Latin gets on.
There's billies is docters an' deein' richt weel
That wis lickit alangside o' me at the squeel.
The lad that taks Learnin' gets roadit for fame –
Bit there's some afa' gypes wi' degrees till their name.
Oh, the Learnin's a blessin', bit tak it fae me,
There's a lot to be learnt besides Learnin'.

A College upbringin' hid Fate haen for me,
Had she gien me the pick o' fit I wis tae be,
It's the robes o' the Law I'd hae taen, or the Claith,
For there's mony a waur scamp than me been in baith.
Aye (says Tammas) the Learnin's a thing that some micht
Had been lots better wintin', an' losh the man's richt;
For the Learnin's a blessin', bit tak it fae me,
There's a lot tae be learnt besides Learnin'!

(1945)

By Linda Jean Rinker

FOR ANNE

Winter persuaded me of the death of apple trees,
Of the indestructibility of ice,
And deprived me finally of deprivation.

This I had thought,
But today spring came blowing from the land
In a breeze steamed in thawed earth,
A breeze brown with the promise of green tomorrow
   growing.
Tonight I will dream of apple-blossoms,
Secure in the memory of next year's autumn
Sharp and sweet in the crisp flesh of apples.

(1965)

SONNET FOR SEPTEMBER

I cannot think it matters, after all,
That I must go and you remain behind..
Surely we know (or are we growing blind?)
That summer fades and withers to the fall.
In what we knew of August we may find
Some warmth to brick our walls against the blast
Of winter days, but nothing known can last
Beyond a few slow tears. And in this mind
I know the part of me that clings so fast
Against your hands is part of me that dies
To seed another love. Only in lies
Is love forever. Yet when this parting's past
And I am wandering where winds may call,
I cannot think it nothing, after all.

(1967)

By Christine M Ritchie

DEMENTIA

She came suddenly
Like a night bird
Flying on the wings of the moon,
Feathery fronds
Blown
In the wind of flight,
Eyes wild,
Strange and shy.
Seeing beyond our light,
Our world's
Dimensions,
Beyond that hospital room.
And we, earthbound,
Myopic, peer,
The moon obscured by pristine walls
And woods
And mountain masses
Of old, familiar bric-a-brac,
Utilised,
Faint, futile hope,
To entice our wild bird back.

(1991)

MYAAV

Yon's a richt name, Myaav,
Fur yon hallyrackit craturs,
Raggity cyaards it fecht n tyauve,
Roch, coontermashious naturs.

It's a richt complainin kin o a soun,
Myaav – nae neen contentit,
Greedy an screichin, divin doon,
Drivin fyowk dementit

Bit fan they're awa heich oot ower i sea,
Ridin i wild win abeen i heavin faem,
Untrammelt speerits, fleein free,
Myaav is a lanely name.

An fan the livin gales wheep up i angert sea
An furl it roon intil a dreid, dark hole,
A grave, win-delvit, ready fur its deid,
Myaav is a lament fur a human soul.

(1991)

97

By Edith Anne Robertson

THE ARTIFICIAL

Now in the foothills, ploughed fields' rosie goon
Favours the colour o the stane o yon Campanile
Trystan her Duomo for evir in Florence toon:
We sclimmed yon tour, I mind weel, a Maybreak mornin,
Ma brither Harry and me when we were weans;
 The seely rays o the rose-reid sun
  Shone on the rose-reid stanes.

Now in the foothills, – kiltan their velvet drills
Hillocks and howes ower, mile on mile, – slitheran fields
O' rose-reid earth travel frae ferm toons and mills
Doon til the moonstane mist adist the sea;
And the mist haps them in her shawls frae a heidlang fa
 Cliff-ower, whaur, in loury dragonish gills
  The drooned tattie-bogles ca.

Now in the foothills wild gulls scraich and croon
Chased frae the white-maned seas by the Gowk Storm,
Syne skaithed wi the steer o the tatter-wallops frae the toon, –
Two lorry loads, – here for potato plantin:
The worms squirm, for the bairnish sea-maws feed
 On them, onwittins or their bit is done,
  Bird and worm 'll be greed.

Ach! The bricht-bonnie birds . . . five, sax, heedzelteerie
In the rows . . . sleepans, are they? Or is 't Progress, giver and thief?
They're deid in the drills! And ilk bird anither bird's dearie!
The artificial it is, the potato manure!
The pizzen's on the worm, and the worm in the sea-maw's wame:
 Ach ma bonnie ones, sae jimp and feerie!
  And was it for yon ye came?

Far ower freely it's strawed; earth canna cope;
Syne we devour it whaur in winter it lowses in the ruits:
Gulls we'd be deid, but mankind has doctor's dope.
Wir years were nearer hevin when the thole-moody horse
Cairtit the gowdie sea-weed frae tide til field;
 Yon was the glisteran mealie crop!
  Yon was the grand yield!

(1959)

By Robin Robertson

DUNNOTTAR CASTLE

Three sides carved by waterstorm,
red rock wealed, riven by the bannered sea;
one side, spurred neck, narrow as the knife
that cut its edge, left it
scarped to nothing.
All sides anger with the bones gone through,
the barrow scabs and stone;
the coiled sky, and everywhere, the birds.

(1980)

By David Rorie

THE DEIL AND JOCK MacNEIL

O siller's gude and siller's braw
　An' poortith ill to thole,
But dear's the price o' gaithert gear
　Gin the price should be your soul.

Sae be ye carle, or be ye caird,
　Or laird o' high degree,
Lay bye the wark ye hae in han'
　An' hearken weel to me,

While I shall tell o' Jock MacNeil,
　A smith o' muckle skill,
O dule an' wae that it cam frae
　His dealin's wi' the Deil!

For Jock had made a compack fell
　An' by't he maun abide,
That gin he were the skeeliest smith
　In a' the country side.

Ten gude lang year to hammer on
　An' blaw his smiddy coal,
Ten gude lang year to gaither gear,
　The Deil should hae his soul.

Ae winter's nicht the flakes o' snaw
　Cam spitterin' doon his lum,
As stiddy rang, nae blythe voice sang,
　Jock wrocht's gin he were dumb.

Nae blythe voice sings as stiddy rings
　When the heart is fu' o' wae;
Nine year an' mair were past, an' noo
　But seven short months to gae.

O, the smiddy door was opened wide
　By the cauld, cauld, weary win',
An' leadin' his mear a bearded man
　An' auld cam stoiterin' in.

'Noo whaur gang ye, ye silly auld man,
　O, whaur gang ye sae late?
The track to the ford is smoored wi' snaw
　An' the ford's a roarin' spate.'

'An' would ye mell wi' my affairs
    Tho' far am I frae hame?
It's miles ayont I bude to be
    Had the auld mear no gane lame.'

'I amna thrang, it taks na lang
    To shoe an auld white mear.
See, pit that feed aneth her heid
    An' sit ye on that chair.

'Noo what be ye, ye silly auld man,
    Noo what be ye to trade?
An' what can ye lay in my han' to pay
    For the shoe that I hae made?'

'A saint am I frae Heaven on high,
    I hinna gowd nor gear,
But I can grant your heart's desire,
    Three wishes ye can speir,
An' wi' the wishes I'll pay ye, smith,
    For the shoein' o' my gude mear.'

'There's a pear-tree oot in the garden there,
    Ye canna see't for snaw,
I wish whae'er may sklim intil't
    Bides till I say "Awa!" '

'A grant, a grant! O menseless wish!
    Wi' fear my heart's opprest,
Twa wishes yet ye hae to speir –
    O, dinna forget the best!'

'D'ye see that chair ye're sittin' on
    Wi' the lang an' gizzened back?
Whae'er sits on't, e'en lat him sit
    Till I bid him rise an' walk!'

Up rose the saint afore he said,
    'O, fule ye stand confest!
Aince mair a grant! But ae wish left!
    Noo dinna forget the best!'

'See, here's a purse het frae my pooch,
    A purse o' linkit chain,
May a' livin' things that creep intil't
    At my biddin' there remain.'

101

'O, I maun rise an' I maun rin
  An' I maun saddle an' ride;
'Tis I maun reach the yetts o' Heaven
  This nicht whate'er betide;
An' ye've tint the best that man can wish
  For the sake o' earthly pride!'

'Twas a braw, braw nicht o' August month
  An' never a breath o' win',
When Jock was switin' ower his wark
  An' the Deil cam danderin' in.

'It's a fine nicht, Jock,' says the muckle black Deil,
  'Ay, a fine nicht, Deil,' says Jock,
'What kin' o' weather has't been doon bye
  An' hoo are a' your folk?'

Auld Hornie girned, 'I hinna come
  For a lang twa-handit crack:
Lay bye that wark ye're warkin' on
  For I maun haste me back.'

'E'en lat me finish this gude horse shoe
  Syne I'm at your command,
An' ye can try thae pears oot-bye
  That's hingin' to your hand.'

'I'll lat ye finish that gude horse shoe
  As ye hae it in hand,
An' I'll slocken my drooth wi' the bonny wee pears
  Till ye're at my command.'

As through the winnock he keekit oot
  Jock saw wi' muckle glee
The Deil eat a' that he could rax,
  Syne sklim intil the tree.

'I hae ye noo, Auld Nickie Ben,
  I hae ye by the horn,
An' the auld pear tree shall be your bed
  Till the cock craws in the morn.'

O, sair the Deil he tried to flit,
  He banned wi' a' his power,
He warsled weel, but ne'er a fit
  Frae the pear tree gat attour.

'Anither ten year, a bargain fair,
    E'er I sit wi' ye in hell;
Shak' hands on't owre the yird-fast stane
    That's stan'in by the well!'

Anither ten year o' gaitherin' gear,
    Anither ten year o' pride,
Jock lookit roon' ae August nicht
    An' the Deil was at his side.

'O, aince again your tack's rin oot,
    O, this time nae denial,
For a full ten year I've gien to ye
    By the shadow on the dial!'

'E'en lat me finish this braw horse shoe
    An' that's a' my demand,
An' ye can try thae pears oot-bye
    That's hingin' to your hand.'

'O, I winna fash wi' pears the nicht,
    I'm some distraucht inside,
I thank ye kindly a' the same,
    But here I'm gaun to bide.'

'The while I finish this braw horse shoe,
    The wark I hae in hand,
Just tak' the chair ye see owre there,
    Ye weel may sit as stand.'

Doon sat the Deil intil the chair
    Wi' the lang and gizzened back,
In sudden fear he strave to rise
    An' never a move could mak.

'I hae ye noo, Auld Nickie Ben,
    I hae ye by the tail,
An' ye shall sit till the dew o' morn
    Pits pearlins on the kale.

'Ye needna flyte, ye needna ban,
    Ye needna rug an' tear,
Till I raise my finger an' bid ye walk
    Ye're thirled till the chair!'

'Anither ten year will I gie ye, Jock,
    Gin ye but set me free,
An' I'll pay ye back at the en' o' your tack
    For the chair an' the auld pear-tree.'

Anither ten year o' gaitherin' gear,
    Anither ten year o' pride,
An' Jock stude still wi' cockit lug
    For he heard the Deil ootside;

Syne yokit till his shoe again
    Wi' dirdum an' wi' din,
But ae ee on the smiddy door
    As the Deil cam sidlin' in.

'Twice hae I come to tak ye, Jock,
    An' twice ten year ye've thieved,
Thrice wi' the glamour o' your tongue
    I winna be deceived!'

'E'en lat me finish this wee horse shoe,
    An' I'm at your command,
An' ye can try thae pears oot-bye
    That's hingin' to your hand.'

'O, fruit's no gangin' wi' my heart
    Nor yet wi' my inside,
I winna say but ye wish me weel
    Yet here I'm gaun to bide!'

'Then while I finish this wee horse shoe,
    Nor yet wi' my inside,
I winna say but ye wish me weel
    Yet here I'm gaun to bide!'

'Then while I finish this wee horse shoe,
    The wark I hae in hand,
What ails ye at the chair owre there –
    Ye weel may sit as stand.'

'My feet are cauld, I winna sit,
    It sets me better to stand,
The time ye finish the wee horse shoe,
    The wark ye hae in hand.'

'O a' men say ye're clever, Deil,
    That unco things ye dae,
Ye can mak yersel' as muckle's ye like –
    Noo tell me, is that sae?'

He's swallowed himsel' an' better swalled
    As the wind blaws oot a sail,
He's swalled himself' an' better swalled
    Till ye couldna see his tail.

He's sookit in air an' he's sookit in reek,
　　He's sookit in soot an' stoor,
Till his horns gaed cracklin' through the roof
　　An' his hurdies through the door.

'Ye winna beat that,' says the muckle black Deil,
　　'Lang, lang although ye try,
I can beat ye there, my skeely smith,
　　An' I'll hae ye yet forbye!'

'Noo for the power to dae siclike
　　I wadna gie a curse,
Lat's see ye mak yersel' as sma'
　　As creep intil this purse!'

Nae horny-golloch is sae sma'
　　As the Deil's noo made himsel,
Intil the purse o' linkit chain
　　He's creepit, heid an' tail.

Jock's snappit the purse o' burnished steel,
　　The purse o' linkit chain,
He's leuch to hear Auld Clootie's squeal
　　To be latten oot again.

'I hae ye noo, Auld Nickie Ben,
　　I hae ye hide an' hair!
An' I'll ding ye harns an' horns an' hoofs,
　　Till ye binna sweir to swear
That aye frae here ye'll bide awa'
　　An' herry me nae mair!'

Wi's hammer he's dung him harns an' hoofs
　　An' horns an' hide an' hair,
Till he's passed his word as Earl o' Hell
　　He'd herry him nae mair.

The lang years passed an' Jock grew auld
　　An' frail an' fu' o' years,
An' ae cauld nicht he soughed awa'
　　Like the lave o' his forebears.

An' when he cam' to the yetts o' Heaven,
　　O, wha is stan'in there,
Wi's lang, lang beard but the silly auld man
　　That aucht the auld white mear.

'Ye needna preach, ye needna fleech,
  Nor mak' nae prayers to me,
For ye didna wish the ae best wish
  When ye were offered three.'

Jock heard it a' an' turned awa'
  An' hooly was his pace,
As he keepit on the weel-trod track
  That leads till the Ill Place.

An' there he saw the yetts set wide,
  Set wide against the wa',
An' Auld Sootie was watchin' his reekit menyie
  A-playin' at the ba'.

The Deil glowered thrice ablow his han'
  When Jock he did espy,
Syne stappit twa fingers in his mou'
  An' whistled them a' in-bye.

He's clashed thegither his iron yetts
  Wi' dirdum an' wi' din,
He's chackit the tails aff a dizen wee deils
  That were late o' scramblin' in.

'Noo, a' my folk they ken ye, Jock,
  Ken ye an' a' your gear,
Sae we're seekin' nae pears an' we're seekin' na chairs,
  An' we're seekin' nae purses here!

'O, ye arena fish an' ye arena flesh
  Nor gude red herrin' are ye,
Wi' the Orra Folk at the Auld Cross Roads
  Is where your stance maun be.'

It's no' a place ye'd ca' a place,
  But he bides there year by year,
In hopes o' pittin' anither shoe
  On Peter's auld white mear.

Sae be ye caird or be ye laird
  Or be ye sick or weel,
Whate'er your kind, O, bear in mind
  The fate o' Jock MacNeil.

For siller's guid an' siller's braw
  An' poortith ill to thole.
But dear's the price o' gaithert gear
  Gin the price should be your soul.

(1925)

By Christopher Rush

IF ONLY YOU WOULD FALL AGAIN INTO MY HEART

If only you would fall again into my heart,
if only you would sweep like the sea into my heart
and drag me down in your sad ports,
ghost-girl of the golden storms.

Years have fallen like cities of trees since we severed,
years have wept like leaves on the wind
and left me lonely and wintered in waste places,
ghost-girl of the wind-torn woods.

I am tired of my loud successes and succession of days,
I am tired of my friends and the fixedness of feet,
and I'm tired, yes tired, of so many places without you,
ghost-girl of my ridiculous youth!

Bright the hooting of boats in the blistering bay,
bright the screams of gulls on forgotten beaches,
and I'm sick for the stars of the hunter over these places,
ghost-girl, in the fogs and squalls of my tears.

I don't want, one day, to be a soul on a lonely shore,
I don't want, one day, to be the spirit of the sea,
all I want, one day, is to sail madly back again,
ghost-girl, to the quiet harbour of your arms.

You held me close under the star-stabbed sky,
you rained wish-kisses like meteors on my mouth,
and your eyes, dear heart, were wide as absence –
ghost-girl, and your voice, my dear, as low as hope.

Your breasts were there for the drinking like goblets of snow,
your tongue a red bell beating against mine,
and the hugeness of seas and the sadness of waves breaking,
ghost-girl, quickened my sudden desire.

My kisses passed like gondolas along your lips,
like red embers wrested by fingers of the tide,
and my hands could hold no longer the torches of your words,
ghost-girl, I dropped them burning into the sea.

Oh, love me again, old friend, companion of past years –
don't leave me to founder on the flood of desire!
where I throw out my frantic net of words,
ghost-girl, to catch you like the drowned moon.

Everything is full of you tonight, the drenched gardens,
the city streets that soak up the headlamps and rain,
and the shining roofs and trains and deserted docks at dawn,
ghost-girl, are heavy with your pale gaze.

Your name is written on the wings of the south wind,
my words dying on your ears like tired geese,
yes, your name tinkles in the copper castles of the trees,
ghost-girl, throbbing in the year's dead-end gale.

The stars shiver like fish in the sky's firth,
hurricanes haul me out of the tents of sleep,
and pibrochs of passion throng the long winter sheets,
ghost-girl, where I freeze to the memory of your touch.

Closeness keeps you distant, but space is shrunk now
to rooms like counties, corn-stacked between us,
and the sentinel gull sits on my chimney top,
ghost-girl, like a sad captain, bearing you away.

Ah, the days flutter to earth, harden and die like anchors,
the planets pass like people over the hills,
and my aching arms reach out like old stone piers,
ghost-girl, cradling the empty waves.

And I'm wild with fear that you'll never be mine again,
ghost-girl, returning forever to another,
and the pen tingles like a duelling sword,
ghost-girl, fired by the true madness of love.

And if these be the last lines I write for you,
ghost-girl, I can see no ending but despair.

(1994)

LINES FOR PATRICIA

A broken creel and the sea on her shoulder –
she closed her eyes and laughed
at the tangled lines that time had told her
all things turn to, unwoven for her fun.
Join with her then, rejoice, be daft
and happy if you dare, hold her,
enfold her, repay that smile. No-one
has her now, her hand, her hair; the boulder
on the beach is more my wife
than this stopped picture of a life
unreachable, a lass unwrinkled in laughter's craft,
too blithe, too young: a woman clothed with the sun.

(1994)

By Glenn Edward Sadler

ACADEMIC REGRET
(For George MacDonald)

Three crowned years it took – alas –
to divide your poet's soul and set
alive in jewelled words a paper rose.

Fragile, blue-white fairies flitted
into brittle thoughts as down their
ruined snowdrop palace scattered
Softly over ink-pools; the white seaside
Venus shut tight her marble lids at
the tap of striking lettered keys.

Outside the window I stood in time,
peeking into your cosmic house,
And saw the repentant child, twisted
at the Father's feet: heard the death-toll
Shatter the granite night into harebells
of black sea-foam, and saw the infant
Dream float silently upward home.

As the mystic film blurred the view,
I erased the dream; set up your floral
vision of sapphire floors and holy blue.

But yet I fear to push the castle-door;
to climb the stairs of timeless spheres
And step inside your cave of brilliant sleep.
Still I hear the North wind's ancient woes
and weep because her magic echoes
Not back in my bound, academic prose.

(1966)

109

By Alexander M Scott

SNOW
A Dialogue with Death

Under the terrible pallor of snow, the earth
Lies colourless and cold as a bleached bone.
A face which death has smoothed of all its wrinkles
(Footpaths, a dawdling stream, a mesh of hedges),
The drifted valley gapes in a blank stare
And trees are skeleton arms in a last anguish
Thrown up to tear and tear the horizon's end.
Alone. I am alone in a dead world
Strangled by the silken garotte of snow.

Dangerous thoughts, said Lancelot Maths-for-the-Million,
With nothing whatever to bore him but football and God.
Steadily now, and emulate Stearns in constructing
Something on which to rejoice, for now if ever
Here is your chance to prove to your doubting self
The truth you have always cried at the doubting world,
That culture (displayed in your habit of apt quotation)
Arms you against outrageous fortune's arrows.
Arrows, you say? Anachronistic error.
The barb you carry festering in your flesh,
Is far more modern, the very latest product
Contrived by the tricks of inexorable progress –
The machine-gun bullet. Quote *that* away, you jester,
You grin on the mouth of a skull, if you can. If you can.

When will they come? How long? Will they never come?
Dawn when he left me, how many hours ago,
How many years, how many centuries?
My watch is broken. A symbol? Quiet, you fool,
Your symbols cannot save you. The flask is empty,
The flask, not bigger than your hand, which lent you
What all your pampered books could not supply –
A little warmth and courage. Empty. Drained
As dry as your heart of hope. And who will help you?
No one. Except yourself. Now sneer at Smiles.
Sit with your back to this crumbling wall and sneer
While your fingers grip the death in your own body
And the blood ticks in your ruined veins like time.

The moonlight glittering over the snow was steel
Stripping the darkness clean of any cover,
So we patrolled towards the enemy
Naked as in the blaze of summer's noon.
The Spandaus chattered, bit the air with bullets.
Floundering down in the snow, we foxes cowered

Deeper away from the death that bayed for our blood.
But snow, as frail as flesh, would not defend us.   .
In the mercurial moonlight blood was black
On the bitter blade of the snow.

Come. Come now. Quickly. Quickly. Quickly.
All was quiet after he left me. Quiet.
The western front, all quiet. Except my heart
Beating, beating, I heard my heart beating,
The knell of parting life. He climbed the hill,
His body leant away from his savaged arm,
And the snow like dust was puffing around his feet
As he stumbled over the crest and escaped my staring.
Then quiet, quiet. I watched the line of light
Broaden across the sky. And not a sound.
I should have heard the shots if luck betrayed him.
But what if he lost the road? He could not lose it,
Could not, could not, straight as a line on a map.
Then why do they not come? Quickly. Quickly.
The snow. It must be the snow. The snow delays them,
Clogging their feet, the lead-weight, dead-weight snow.

Right then, you faker with words, you fiddler with phrases,
Whistle me up a word or a phrase for the snow.
'Conciseness. Clarity. These are the two essentials
Of any work of art.' Be clear and concise, then,
Find me a word for the snow. You have *carte blanche*
(*Toujours la langue française, toujours l'amour*)
To rummage the Ancient World, to plunder the classics,
Or filch from the cliques, the dead-and-alive, the living,
The cliques whose cosiness you envy often.
Quickly, you forger of fancies, coin me a word,
A word for the snow, a word for your own death.
Judas.

So ho, you shoddy Voltaire, you erstwhile darer
Of all the unknown, when *timor mortis* appals you
You squeal like a rabbit and bolt for the Bible's burrow!
Too late, that hole is long since stopped with stones
You carried there yourself, your flinty jibings.
Remember, man made God in his own image,
And what we moderns wish immaculate
Is contraception, not conception. *Contra*,
The modern prefix. Against. Against. Against.

The snow was against us all, against us all.
That whey-faced quisling whose only delight is treason
Betrayed our approach to the pointed muzzles of guns
But then, while the bullets snarled for the final kill,
Cheated their lust, denied their seemingly certain

Consummation of slaughter. The blizzard's fury,
Suddenly pouncing, blinded and gagged the guns,
And through that smother of snow we crawled to shelter,
Two of us, bleeding, torn by the teeth of wounds.
The rickle of ruined walls we reached at last
Was meagre safety, yet I could go no farther.
Agony burned in my blood at every step,
Pain was a fire that utterly consumed
My scanty crop of courage. Here, the harvest
Flared in a puff of smoke like straw and fell,
A litter of useless ash. And here he left me,
My failure propped against the fallen rubble,
To go alone across that desert of snow
And find our friends, to find our friends and bring them
Back into danger that my helplessness
May even yet be carried into safety.

What friends have you, my whimpering crusader,
That are not safe a thousand miles or more
From this one point where history and fate
Converge in action or disappear in death?
Long since, in another, easy-osey world
Of books and talk, books and talk, you chose
Your comrades in arms (the elegant arms of the Muses),
Campaigners on paper who captured a word or a line,
Conquered a sentence, or took a verse by storm.
Cable them now and back they will send by return
The latest in elegies, proving beyond all cavil
That typewriter chatter is more than a match for
                                        machine-guns.
No, it is not your friends you pray for now
To come, O quickly, come now, quickly, come,
But the uniformed oafs, those readers of penny dreadfuls
Whose lecherous glee at Miss Blandish's lack of orchids
Offended your own delight in the Iron Laurel,
The boors whose talk was forever of wine and women
(Brothels and beer), the half-illiterate gang
Who grumbled over the grub but never mentioned
Terror and death – the soldiers, the scapegoat soldiers
Who carry the whole intolerable weight
Of crumbling civilisation upon their backs
And scarcely know it. Those are the new messiahs
You long for now, the lechers, the oafs, the boors,
The ignorant saviours, the unheroic heroes.

But you in childhood never would play at soldiers,
Preferring to sit at dusk in the quivering firelight
That crimsoned the air like a warm September vintage
And listen, intent, to your favourite fairytale:
'The Snow King came and carried them all away

112

To the Frozen Land. As huge as a winter pine,
His beard a cataract of ice, his eyes
Glittering frost, the Snow King came and carried
Them all away to the Frozen Land.' You listened,
Catching your breath while there, beyond the windows,
The single flakes came fluttering lightly down
And banded together to bury the earth in snow.

But the earth endures beneath the snow till springtime,
Endures as the rock the ceaseless grind of the sea
And the sea the endless stubborn repulsion of rock,
Action and then reaction and quiet never.
Endure. Only endure. Endure to the end.

Darling, my love, my lovely, held and holding
– The snow grins with a flash of glistening fangs –
April was in the candour of your eyes
–But the whistle blew, the train shuddered and shuddered,
I lost you, lost in the platform's narrowing blur.

Dancing, dancing, always I think of us dancing,
The light in pools on the ballroom's glittering floor,
The partners swooping, pausing, poised, and swirling
In suddenly flaring arcs of taffeta foam,
And laughter, always an incandescence of laughter,
Brighter than any moonlight ever snow.

But now the blizzard breaks above the dancing,
The lights go out like snuffed candles, the snow
Smothers the glittering floor, the easy dancers
Drown in a white sea, a flood of frost
Where the sinews freeze, the heart goes beating backward,
The blood retreats in its running, the flesh is stone.
Endure like stone. Endure. Endure. Endure.

I am foundered within a whelming ocean of ice,
And time and chance are waves that drive me farther
Away and forever away from your love's island.

The sun splits in the snow.
Endure what anger?
Huge as a winter pine,
His beard a cataract of ice, his eyes
Glittering frost. Glittering.
Glittering.

(1946)

113

By John Watt Simpson

'ILIUM'

Fair was your city, old and fair,
And fair the Hall where the Kings abode,
And you speak to us in your despair,
To us who see but ruins bare,
A crumbled wall, a shattered stair,
And graves on the Menin Road.

It was sweet, you say, from the City Wall
To watch the fields where the horsemen rode:
It was sweet to hear at evenfall
Across the moat the voices call:
It was good to see the stately Hall
From the paths by the Menin Road.

Yea, Citizens of the City Dead,
Whose souls are torn by memory's goad:
But now there are stones in the Cloth Hall's stead,
And the moat that you loved is sometimes red,
And the voices are still, and laughter sped,
And torn is the Menin Road.

And by the farms and the House of White,
And the shrine where the little candle glowed,
There is silence now by day and night,
Or the sudden crash and the blinding light,
For the guns smite ever as thunders smite,
And there's death on the Menin Road.

(1916)

114

By Thomas Sinton

HERACLITUS

Εἶπέ τις, Ἡράκλειτε, τεὸν μόρον, ἐς δέ με δάκρυ
ἤγαγεν, ἐμνήσθην δ' ὁσσάκις ἀμφότεροι
ἠέλιον λέσχῃ κατεδύσαμεν. ἀλλὰ σὺ μέν που,
ξεῖν' Ἁλικαρνησσεῦ, τετράπαλαι σποδιή
αἱ δὲ τεαὶ ζώουσιν ἀηδόνες, ᾗσιν ὁ παντων
ἁρπακτὴρ Ἀΐδης οὐκ ἐπὶ χεῖρα βαλεῖ.

— CALLIMACHUS

They told me, Heraclitus, they told me you were dead,
They brought me bitter news to hear and bitter tears to shed.
I wept, as I remembered how often you and I
Had tired the sun with talking and sent him down the sky.

And now that thou art lying, my dear old Carian guest,
A handful of grey ashes, long, long ago at rest,
Still are thy pleasant voices, thy nightingales, awake;
For Death, he taketh all away, but them he cannot take.

— WILLIAM CORY

Chaidh ìnnseadh dhomh, a Dhunnachaidh, mo nuar! nach 'eil thu beò,
'S gu 'm b'airsnealach an sgialachd sin a lìon mmo shùil le deòir.
Do ghuil mi 's mi bhi cuimhneach' liuthad comhra bh' againn riamh,
'S cia tric bha 'ghrian air bodhradh leinn, is ruaig sinn i do 'n iar.

Ach nis, gu 'm beil thu 'd shìneadh, a charaid chaomhail chòir,
Mar dhuslach anns an ùir-thigh far nach fhaicear thu ni's mò;
Tha fonn do ghuth gun sguir 'n a dhùisg mar chomh-sheirm bhinn
nan ian;
Gu 'n glac an t-Eug gach nì bu leam, ach mairidh so do shìor.

(1920)

By George Adam Smith

OLD ABERDEEN, OCTOBER, 1915

Mother of trees and towers and ancient ways
   And homes of studious peace; to whose grey Crown
Thy lads come up through these October days,
   Come up again the while thy leaves fall down –
Rustling about the young and eager feet,
   As if the spirits of thy crowded past,
Mustering on high those latest ranks to greet,
   Did down their ghostly salutations cast –

Ah, this October many come no more,
   Whose trysted faces we had looked to see,
For on the fields of Flanders or that shore,
   Steep and fire-swept, of grim Gallipoli,
They fell like leaves, innumerably fell,
   And, though still quick and keen and fain for life,
With as ripe ease and gentleness of will,
   As the sere leaf from out the tempest's strife –
Ready for Death and their young sacrifice
   By faith in God, by love of home and land,
And the proud conscience of the ungrudged price
   Their fathers paid at Freedom's high demand.

Though through thy stripped trees, trailing with the mist
   The mournful music of the pipes comes creeping,
Mourn thou not those who only failed thy tryst
   Because they kept a holier – and are keeping.

                                (1935)

By Harry Smith

'THE THING THAT'S DEEN'

Noo, tak' yer buiks an' learn yer wark,
    An' nae ae ither wird be said:
Gey-like to play till gloamin'-dark
    An' syne be ready for yer bed!
That's nae the wye to maister ocht –
Ye're aul' aneuch to hae mair thocht;
Foo gar me threip on't ilka day –
It's first yer wark an' syne yer play?

'The morn's mornin'' did I hear?
    Some fowk's owre fond o' that doon-sit;
Nae won'er they're aye in a steer,
    Aye plowter-plowt'rin' i' the bit!
The sweer wye they pit aff's nae mowse –
Afore they're yok't it's time to lowse.
Ye canna lippen to the morn –
Wi' lippen'd ploos ye saw nae corn.

The morn, awat, gin't gie's a ca',
    'Ull hae 'ts nain trokes for you an' me;
Sae tak' this tellin', eence for a', –
    The thing that's deen is nae adee.
Fat eese noo is't to glunch an' glower?
Ye'd best sit doon an' get it owre:
Sae come yer wa's, yer lessons learn,
An' nae grow up a glaiket bairn.
  . . . .

It's forty, fifty year, an' mair,
    Sin my wyce mither dreel't me weel.
I've wan'ert far, an' trauchlet sair,
    An' got my licks in life's hard skweel;
Bit wi' her wirds stoups to my he'rt
I've warstl't throw an' deen my pairt;
I daur haud up my heid the day
By pittin' wark afore my play.

An' gin, forby, I played or vrocht,
    I tried to min' my '*Man's chief en*' ';
To ser' my Maister aye I socht
    An' on His blessin' to depen'.
Baith wark an' play are noo near by –
Gin they be a', then fat hae I?
Bit I've made pac' 'tweesh Him an' me –
That's ae thing deen that's nae adee.

(1922)

117

By Iain Crichton Smith

ONLY THE SEA REMAINS

Only the sea remains; the pinched faces
On the promenades are mere film-shots
Eliminated by a wink in the biting wind.
All walkers hurry to eternity,
See death in the flamboyant windows, in
The man at the corner with the shaded hat.
O desolation of peoples,
Moving in a drift of water, caught
In the tough tangle and the spidery masts,
I also seek protection from the thrust
Of the waves, ignore the cap and the bonnet
Tossed on the shaggy beaches.
I also lean to the wall when the wind
Breaks with a flurry of feathers
And Island reminiscences.

Only the sea remains; all monuments subside,
Are bitten by time. Migrations of people
Stir in the sad morning, wingless birds
For whom nothing is important or durable.
The shadow falls on the foreshore:
But O that this moment were halted
And the seagull strayed in the sunset,
Confident in the unfiring gun and the easy heavens:
And the crowds would find by the seaside
The miracle of faith,
The stranger in the ultimate boat;
Only the sea remains,
And my heart is sad for my people
Whose common denominator is death
And birth, beside a timeless sea.

(1948)

118

RETURN TO ABERDEEN UNIVERSITY

Thirty six years afterwards I return.
Everyone's so young. The days of iron
soften intently towards my youth again.

when I was one of those who sparked my wit
in loose cheap blazer along Union Street
and the moony chimes struck heavily through the night.

So young, so young! The cinemas are gone,
replaced by bingo. The theatre remains
refurbished in gold leaf and Cupid wings.

Remember me. I strolled in Hazlehead
when the autumn leaves were golden overhead
and girls with cracked handbags giggled down the street.

The statues were imperious, overblown.
In bare religious Lewis there were none,
only the justice of the windswept stone.

Bookshops and churches, buses, study rooms.
There is a play of wavering white flames.
We have lived since then through the most violent times,

but the quadrangles remain quiet as once before.
I push (extraordinarily) this well-known door.
I am an explorer but what I explore

is the past not present. The professors change,
the lecturers are bearded, young and strange.
At fifty seven to casually range

the roads of yesterday seems eerie now.
Time eats us momently. Paunchy, middle brow,
how can I face the idealist I knew

intense, self-conscious. Or how justify
the choices and the failures? Oh, we die
so many times, on our concessive journey.

This is a resurrection and a death.
Pale ghost, I love you, but your venomous breath
would kill me now, I think. Not all the earth

is possible imperium, I say.
I am the Roman of another day
the gaunter copy of a vast Idea,

Platonic and autumnal. Let me live.
Do not condemn me to another grave
but take me by the hand. O please forgive

your elder and your senior. Be polite.
Open the doors for me. Give up your seat,
my blazing adolescent. Don't repeat

old jokes about me. Do not mock or scorn.
You also had your days of smoke and iron.
You also had a life (not book) to learn

and saw the leaves deceive you, become frayed.
You also were by marble speech betrayed,
the adamantine proverbs of the dead.

So let us walk together down this street,
a father and a son perhaps, in light
of supernatural clarity and granite

sparkling with a memory and a present fire.
The cobblestones are shaky. O for fear
that we fail or falter let us walk together

in the common merciful air so bright and green
in ancient solid vanishing Aberdeen.

(1987)

120

By Alan D Stuart

MEMORIES

Memories are where we live,
Run in the flickering,
Dumb-shows of the mind;
Run and re-run, edit and focus,
An endless silent arabesque.

(1988)

SEAGULLS

Here on my back,
Seagulls drift into my grey quartered world
of window
– Sink deep into the oblongs of light,
Float upward, then are tugged away.

Clear grey curves of grace;
My ideals soar – defined,
No longer earthbound,
Thin and delicate, yet fresh,
In the new, clear glass.

Now one glides into the old pane;
And viewed through the flaws,
A ripple steals through the reflections,
Of my self communings.

Amorphous concepts with wings,
– Immediately aged.
Distorted, diffuse and indistinct –
Viewed through tears.

(1988)

A SHIRT BOX TIED WITH TWINE

A shirt box tied with twine,
Crammed with the paper memories
of my father's maiden aunt;
herself a palsied half memory
of an antique woman
nursed to her death
by my youthful mother.
– a deprivation of attention
in those endless, bantling noons.

Dozens of tiny, stiff photographs
of grey and brown – colourless.
Sepia sunlight on ceremental flesh,
And a feeling of irreverence at
the realisation she had a figure.

Gentle eyes focus on some infinite point,
– look out, time is vague.

Unidentified relations and friends
at a large congregational picnic –
Girls sweltering in yards of material,
the men, moustached, waistcoated
and wearing hats,
with Passchendaele in their eyes.
A small earnest boy sits
crosslegged with an accordion,
washed with grubby shadows,
amidst fossilised grasses.

What was it that was missing
as I rummaged through
these siccative, unleavened scraps?
This new discovered girl did not age
beyond perhaps twenty.

Till suddenly in sharp contrast,
it was her, silver haired,
features blurred,
receiving a retirement radio
from fellow workers in the sixties.

Some hand-tinted postcards
of seaside towns, never sent.
Small exercise journals of her holidays
in this missing middle age.
Modest little stays
with accommodating relatives
in those optimistic postcard resorts
of the fifties.

Months preserved in the spartan posterity
of lists.
– the highlights, a cream-tea
or an accompanied visit to the pictures.

Then at the bottom of the debris,
the answer, perhaps
to this solitary existence;
the story behind the engraved bracelet
given to my mother on that last,
long afternoon.
– a black-edged Mass card
picturing a strong-looking young man
with black passionate eyes.

What sort of life,
summarised by fragments in a box of card?
What choice?
All is past that was permanent,
The impermanent survives us.

(1991)

By Mary Symon

THE GLEN'S MUSTER ROLL
The Dominie loquitur:

Hing't up aside the chumley-cheek, the aul' glen's Muster Roll,
A' names we ken fae hut an' ha', fae Penang to the Pole,
An' speir na gin I'm prood o't – Losh! coont them line by line,
Near han' a hunner fechtin' men, an' they a' were Loons o' Mine.

A' mine. It's jest like yesterday they sat there raw on raw,
Some tchyauvin' wi' the 'Rule o' Three,' some widin' throw 'Mensa':
The Map o' Asia's shoggly yet faur Dysie's sheemach head
Gied cleeter-clatter a' the time the carritches was said.
'A limb,' his greetin' granny swore, 'the aul' deil's very limb' –
But Dysie's dead an' drooned lang syne; the *Cressy* coffined him.
'Man guns upon the fore barbette!' . . . What's that to me an' you?
Here's moss an' burn, the skailin' kirk, aul' Kissach beddin's soo.
It's Peace, it's Hame, – but ower the Ben the coastal searchlights shine,
And we ken that Britain's bastions mean – that sailor Loon o' Mine.

The muirlan's lang, the muirlan's wide, an' fa says 'ships' or 'sea'?
But the tang o' saut that's in wir bleed has puzzled mair than me.
There's Sandy wi' the birstled shins, faur think ye's he the day?
Oot where the hawser's tuggin' taut in the surf o' Suvla Bay;
An' ower the spurs o' Chanak Bahr gied twa lang, stilpert chiels
I think o' flappin' butteries yet, or weyvin' powets' creels –
Exiles on far Australian plains, but the Lord's ain boomerang
'S the Highland heart that's aye for hame hooever far it gang.
An' the winds that wail ower Anzac an' requiem Lone Pine
Are nae jest a' for stranger kin, for some were Loons o' Mine.

They're comin' hame in twas an' threes: there's Tam fae Singapore –
Yon's his, the string o' buckie-beads abeen the aumry door –
An' Dick Macleod, his sanshach sel' (Guid sake, a bombardier!)
I see them yet ae summer day come hodgin' but the fleer:
'Please, sir' (a habber an' a hoast) – 'Please, sir' (a gasp, a gulp,
Syne wi' a rush) 'Please – sir – can – we – win – oot – to – droon – a –
     fulp?
. . . Hi Rover, here lad! – ay, that's him, the fulp they didna droon,
But Tam – puir Tam lies cauld an' stiff on some gray Belgian dune;
An' the Via Dolorosa's there, faur a wee bit cutty quine
Stan's lookin' doon a teem hill-road for a sojer Loon o' Mine.

Fa's neist? The Gaup – a Gordon wi' the 'Bydand' on his broo,
Nae murlacks dreetlin' fae his pooch, or roon the weeks o's mou',
Nae word o' groff-write trackies on the 'Four best ways to fooge' –
He steed his grun' an' something mair, they tell me, oot at Hooge.
But ower the dyke I'm hearin' yet: 'Lads, fa's on for a swap?
A lang sook o' a pandrop for the sense o' 'verbum sap'.

Fack's death I tried to min' on't – here's my gairten wi' the knot –
But – bizz! – a dhûbrack loupet as I passed the muckle pot.'
Ay, ye didna ken the classics, never heard o' a co-sine,
But here's my aul' lum' aff to ye, dear gowket Loon o' Mine.

They're handin' oot the halos, an' three's come to the glen –
There's Jeemack taen his Sam Browne to his mither's but an' ben.
Ay, they ca' me 'Blawin' Beelie,' but I never crawed sae crouse
As the day they ga' the V.C. to my filius nullius.
But he winna sit 'Receptions,' nor keep on his aureole,
A' he says is, 'Cut the blether, an' rax ower the Bogie Roll'.
An' the Duke an's dother shook his han' an' speirt aboot his kin,
'Old family, yes: here sin' the Flood,' I smairtly chippet in,
(Fiech! Noah's? Na – We'd ane wirsels, ye ken, in '29).
I'm nae the man to stan' an' hear them lichtlie Loon o' Mine.

Wir Lairdie. That's his mither in her doo's-neck silk gaun' by,
The podduck, sae she tells me, 's haudin' up the H.L.I.
An' he's stan'in ower his middle in the Flanders clort an' dub –
Him 'at eese't to scent his hanky an' speak o's mornin' 'tub'.
The Manse Loon's dellin' divots on the weary road to Lille,
An' he canna flype his stockin's, 'cause they hinna tae nor heel.
Sennelager's gotten Davie – a' mou' fae lug to lug –
An' the Kaiser's kyaak, he's writin', 'll neither ryve nor rug.
'But mind ye' (so he post-cairds) 'I'm already ower the Rhine.'
Ay, there's nae a wanworth o' them, though they werena Loons o' Mine.

. . . You – Robbie. Memory pictures: Front bench. A curly pow,
A chappet hannie grippin' ticht a Homer men't wi' tow –
The lave a' scrammelin' near him like bummies roon a bike,
'Fat's this?' 'Fat's that?' He'd tell them a' – ay, speir they fat they like,
My hill-foot lad! A' sowl an' brain fae's bonnet to his beets,
A 'Fullarton' in posse – nae the first fun' fowin' peats.
An' I see a blythe young Bajan gang whistlin' doon the brae,
An' I hear a wistful Paladin his patriot Credo say.
An' noo, an' noo I'm waitin' till a puir thing hirples hame –
Ay 't 's the Valley o' the Shadow, nae the mountain heichts o' Fame.
An' where's the nimble nostrum, the dogma fair an' fine,
To still the ruggin' heart I hae for you, oh Loon o' Mine?
  .   .   .   .
My Loons, my Loons! Yon winnock gets the settin' sun the same,
Here's sklates an' skailies, ilka dask a' futtled wi' a name.
An' as I sit a vision comes: Ye're troopin' in aince mair,
Ye're back fae Aisne an' Marne an' Meuse, Ypres an' Festubert;
Ye're back on weary, bleedin' feet – you, you that danced an' ran –
For every lauchin' loon I kent I see a hell-scarred man.
Not mine but yours to question now! You lift unhappy eyes –
'Ah, Maister, tell's fat a' this means.' And I, ye thocht sae wise,
Maun answer wi' the bairn words ye said to me langsyne:
'I dinna ken, I dinna ken,' Fa does, oh Loons o' Mine?

(1915)

125

By Rachel Annand Taylor

BALLAD SONG OF WEST AND EAST
To Sylvia

I

There is a lake of emerald
Within the Isle of Skye:
There is a breaking Western Wave
Will haunt me till I die.

Yet shall not I with dreaming lids
    Drift with the tidal West
That sets in foam of lilies round
    Dim borders of the Blest.

My roots were set in that North-East
    Where ironies prevail;
And Viking white and Norman Knight
    Have grappled with the Gael.

And arrogant songs of wild forebears
    I drank with mother's milk –
Of ballad-barons, Jacobites,
    A folk of steel and silk.

On stones that brood about our fields
    The snake and apple coil;
The merle that flutes the soul away
    Is snared in a strong toil.

We were the Archer Guard of France;
    We read the books of Greece;
We saw on banks beyond the sea
The white lilies grow in Italy,
    And found a great dispeace.

Some merchantmen may gather gear,
    Some scholars flaunt a name.
The best of us love hopeless things
    And die in their own dark flame.

(*There is a lake of emerald*
    Ringed with the hills of Skye:
There is a breaking Western Wave
    Will haunt me till I die.)

126

II

Ah! Where the amber river ran
  With freshets white as curds,
Once Love and Death rode knee to knee
  Across the redding fords,
Twin-bright as golden Gilderoy,
  Flashing Ferrara swords.

Like iris blue and iris white
  Sprang castles French and fair.
It fell about the Martinmas
  The fiery foe was there.
When winds blew cold, like torches burned
  Those castles French and fair.

The adders slither gold and black
  Among the heather bells:
Great fireballs dance the woody rim
  Where the dark thunder dwells:
Strange gods have left in forest-glades
  The panic of their spells.

But sweetly still the river runs
  Its molten amber way,
While green and blue the dainty birks
  Dream through ethereal spray –
'Tis now a murmuring lullaby,
  That scarlet yesterday.

In silvered mail and violet
  The salmon leaps the linn:
And honeybreathing drowse the moors,
  The wild thyme woven in:
The outlaw dead run starred and wild
  With briar and eglantine.

A coven of white foxglove peals
  Faint dirges through the trees;
And rare wood-orchis lingers lone
  In delicate reveries –
As when the great Gauvain rode by
  From his Orcadian seas.

To secret boughs, by magic white
  Cream-pale raspberries cling.
Gold fillets with green beryl drip
  And silver bridles ring:
Queen Marie, or some sister-Fay,
  Lights by a crystal spring.

(There is a rune of Western waves
That charms this heart of mine: –
And yet, by God, in our North-East
They drank a redder wine.)

III

Besieged with waters stands the Town,
    Bleaker than when of old
Wild banners and bells of festival
    Beat the green air to gold.

Since a Waste Land so fierce and fair
    Seemed sore in need of Greek,
A golden Pope, his smooth white hand
    Gemmed with a sard antique,

Read over his Renaissance bull: –
    With seals and silken ties
He sent it to a golden King
    With Flodden in his eyes.

So here arose a calm Crown-Tower,
    And here, with kindling soul,
Came boys to starve and die for Greek,
    While madness took its toll.

And here, to see young Gordon's end
    They brought Queen Marie's grace:
Her long fine fingers gripped the chair
    Over the market-place.

Gone, gone the Chantry by the Brig,
    Madonna silver-gilt,
Gone Magnus Colvin's plaintive bell
    And interceding lilt

For souls in trouble. Troubled still
    Between the Don and Dee,
They craze, aspire, they love and hate
    Like Este, Medici.

Have I not loved thy lovely masks
    Great Athens, Florence, Rome,
Because in Scotland's dark-red flame
    I make my lasting home?

(There is a cry of wild white swans
Between the Night and Day:
There is a challenge in my blood
That bids me stand and stay.)

(1944)

By A L Thomson

LAMENT FOR A HIGHLANDER
A friend dead in battle long ago

He died too young to be remembered,
'mid the vast total of our battle dead,
save by his friends.

We who came through that first world war,
and still survive, have lived well o'er
three times his span.

We scarce recall those trenches, the passing bullet's
whiplash crack, the 'crumping' of a shell,
and death beside us.

And at night th' opposing lines snaked into distance,
each marked by the rocket rise and fall
of watchful lights;

In a boding silence, now and then a shell-burst –
like an avalanche breaking the frost of Alpine dark
with sudden roar.

Ah, the kilt's proud swing, the pipes' fierce skirl,
and the panache of a close-knit body
of fighting men.

These things we shared with those who fell.
Since then we've worked and played with oft
much younger friends.

Yet the lost companion lives in memory of days
when we breasted the hill together, exulted
in the eagle's soar.

(1977)

By Derick Thomson (Le Ruaraidh MacThòmais)

FEVER
Translated from the Gaelic of John MacCodrum's 'Oran do'n
Teasaich'

I came off worse in the wrestling round
I held with the hag, for I'll be bound
she sapped my strength, though I thought it sound,
and laid me flat on my back on the ground.
        My flesh and blood she drained away
        and sent a wheeze in my chest to stay;
        a luckless tryst we had that day;
        God's vengeance smite her without delay.

She planted confusion in my head:
a host of men, both alive and dead,
like those whom the Trojan Hector led,
and Roman warriors thronged my bed;
        that dismal, dark and hunch-backed crone,
        to scandal and lying tales too prone,
        reduced my speech to delirious moan
        and left me, stripped of sense, alone.

What a wretched autumn you've given me,
the harvest's lost, as all can see;
I'm bruised and ill, as here I lie,
with tired bones, and head awry:
        my bones were weary to the core,
        lopped off they'd hardly have hurt more;
        a raging thirst had tried me sore,
        I'd have drained a river from shore to shore.

The fever bed is a wretched place,
you grow lanky and grizzled apace,
shaky and weak, without a trace
of hair on your head, but too much on your face:
        the loathsome beard that you have to wear
        makes your mouth unsavoury; if you dare
        to eat or drink, the lion's share
        of the victuals comes a cropper there.

Your coat has grown too big, and throws
into relief your wrinkled hose,
your splayed, pathetic ankle shows,
long as wild-cat's the nails of your toes,
        bandy legs that fever has made
        pithless, and strengthless thighs – I'm afraid
        they're less like the oar-shaft than the blade –
        if grass but touched them they'd bend and fade.

130

Your scraggy neck is long; you feel
your ribs protrude like the ribs of a creel;
your strengthless hams make it hard to kneel:
your wobbly knees begin to peel
  with rubbing together; the knee-cap's sharp
  and the skin of the knees is as black as bark;
  frightened of cold as a cat – a mark
  that it's time Death folded you in its sark.

Your bonnet seems to have doubled its size,
and it sits on your wig in unsightly wise;
your sprouting ears would win a prize;
what cruel friends could thus devise
  a pate as bald as the palm of the hand
  and a body as thin as a willow wand –
  There's nothing like it in this land:
  Death has enrolled you in its band.

You lurch and sway like a wicket-gate;
the one knee hardly knows its mate;
you're starved of food but easy to sate;
though you haven't taken a drop, your fate
  is to look like a drunkard, a poor mite
  preaching peace since you can't fight,
  in action taking no delight,
  sickly and wan, a sorry sight.

(1963)

SMUAINTEAN ANN AN CAFE AN GLASCHU

A iomallan Burma a bha iad,
òg, brèagh, is gàir' air am bilean dealbhach,
pògan tais na grèin' orra fhathast
an dèidh buige a' mhonsoon,
ceòl mìn nach togadh mo chluasan ceart,
's bha beagan coibhneis 'na mo chridhe riutha –
thuig mi cho duilich 's a tha e dhan S.E.D.
iarrtasan nan Gaidheal a thuigsinn.

THOUGHTS IN A GLASGOW CAFE

From distant Burma they were,
young, lovely, with laughter on their shapely lips,
the sun's soft kisses on them still
after the moistness left by the monsoon,
a delicate music my ears could not properly hear,
and I felt some kindness towards them in my heart –
I understood how difficult it is for the S.E.D.
to understand the Gaels' wishes.

(1987)

By A Christopher Tucker

UWAY TAY EIBURDEEN

A screen to the blasting screams of the North Sea
Lay Aberdeen in wait for me, daring to travel north.

On that blessèd morn, the freeze licked my cheeks
'Till, reaching the kirk, unknown friends greeted me,
loading my inner body with scones and tea, feeding
                    the weary, hungry traveller.

On that very eve sat I by a fire,
Where wee Gabi wound her arms around me
Keeping warm the lonely traveller.

But further north,
Fetterangus greeted my ears with lovely song;
Yea, she sang for me,
    The kind lady,
    The lady wi' the tree
Gladdening me, a waking northern traveller.

                                        (1977)

By Thea Walker

HAPPY NOSTALGIA

It's mair nor fifty year sin' syne,
Fan I wis bit a sonsy quine
An' walkit through the Aul' Toon,
A Bajanella in ma scarlet goon –
(Mebbe a bittie feart for a' that
O' meetin' some stray beast frae the Cattle Mart!)
Gotten tae King's, I attended classes
Alang wi' lands as weel as lasses.
I hearkened hard tae Bonus Bill an' A. A. Jack
(A rhyme for him's nae easy an' that's a fac')
Prof. Terry and a' thae ilk that had a say
In gettin' me cappit a prood M.A.
The Chapel is a quiet an' holy place,
Fu' o' history an' God's guid Grace,
An' those wha, like me, are still aroon
Hae oor cherished memories o' King's aul' croon,
The Library hush wi' tall Miss Broon,
The hops and smokers and Gala Do's
An' a' the dramas o' oor calla' lo'es –
The memories o' it a' are crystal clear,
Fegs aye, far mair nor those o' yester-year.

(1977)

By Roderick Watson

WINTERCLIMB
To Hugh MacDiarmid

'I ken these islands each inhabited
  Forever by a single man.'

1

An easy walk to the ridge on a day
that makes round stones ring
and each footprint a Chinese signature
to set on the white fields below.

Until every extra metre sears the lungs:
kicking steps out of snow   in a long
and ragged slanting line across the hill
exhausting memory   blow by blow

lifting and leaving another step behind
grinding 'you' back   crushing 'me' down   (no song
but a heatless conflagration of the mind)
I drive my boots into the edge. . . .

2

And came to rest by the black cairn.
Without words   and almost beyond sight
I watched the Pentland hills split apart
under the sun and its subtle wedge.

While the day faded to a brittle print
colour of dead grass   under an actinic light
that pierced the bones of my hand   and flared
like gas   from the snow-line on the ridge.

3

The air is so cold.   My legs are uncertain
on the difficult ground.   But at this height
above the town   only distance falls
gently between   us like a bridge.

(1973)

By William Watson

TO ABERDEEN

At the great dance and upleap of the year
    I came. For me, the northwind's cold accost
    Was all day long in thy warm welcome lost.
How should I fail henceforth to hold thee dear?
Hoary thy countenance and thy mien severe,
    And built of the bones of Mother Earth thou wast.
    But on thy heart hath fall'n no touch of frost,
O city of the pallid brow austere.
Grey, wintry-featured, sea-throned Aberdeen!
    The stranger thou hast honoured shall not cease,
    In whatsoever ways he rest or roam,
To wish thee noble fortune, fame serene:
    Thee and thy towers of learning and of peace,
    That brood benignant on the northern foam.

(1935)

By Lord Wavell

A BALLADE OF BEREAVEMENT
DUISBURG: *Amalgamation Day*, 1948

Time was when I was happy and serene
    And mocked at all who thought themselves ill-starred;
Now poltergeists and gremlins intervene
    To haunt and hoist me with my own petard.
My visit to the Regiment is marred
By a disaster not to be foreseen:
    Timor mortis conturbat, sang the bard –
I left my shaving-brush at Aberdeen.

My morning lather is a might-have-been,
    My shaving-soap is like a lump of Lard,
My razor is a mockery (though keen) –
    I might as well have used a Pictish shard.
The harmony of life is sadly marred,
My face has lost its usual ruddy sheen,
    My stubbled cheeks are cicatriced and scarred –
I left my shaving-brush at Aberdeen.

My chin, once glossy as a nectarine,
    Now looks like holly on a Christmas card,
Or straggly hawthorns in a woodland scene
    Such as is deftly drawn by Fragonard;
No R.S.M. would pass me for a Guard
However much I titivate and preen.
    My luck would daunt a Roland or Bayard:
I left my shaving-brush at Aberdeen.

Pity me, Prince: the water here is hard,
    Hourly my tongue inclines to the obscene,
Full of strange oaths and bearded like the pard
    I left my shaving-brush at Aberdeen.

(1948)

By Kenneth Wood

IN MEMORIAM EDWIN MUIR

Quiet under the beeches glides the river.
The smoke of chimneys rises fingering
The evening sky, and you a solitary figure
Among the unkempt grasses walk by the water
With mild and wondering demeanour, while
The woods talk on their whispered talk.
What poem clothes you now? Would it were ours
Transfiguring the timeless rhythm of the land
Our heritage, our cradle, our enchanted source.
Man the wanderer, settler in ancient places,
Whose free inalienable part in things
You ever sang, and the old dream glittered
Like firelight on listening faces.
This we have lost, but will remember long
In the swing of time, touched by the song,
Part of a world peopled by kings,
Alive in a world of wonder at so many graces;
On man and miraculous animals a poet shedding
A great illumination from the flame within,
So gentle, quiet as the moonlight, wedding
Symbol and substance indissolubly, divining
The open right and the hidden wrong. Spin
Still the old Orkney wheel, forever twining
The thread of time from the green isle lying
Over the blue sound with the surf flying,
To make the timeless pictures of the mind.
You are with us still; nor dead, nor dying
Your boundless love for wandering mankind.

(1964)

THE BROCHS OF GLENELG

Silent they stand, two towers in the glen,
Made for forgotten perils so long gone
That here their being's inconceivable.
Deserted. In this rock-strewn domain
The buzzards wheel interminably on
While daylight yet defeats the mist;
And waterfalls their branchy fingers twist
Into the mountain's heart to seek the stone.

The introspective towers captivate the mind
That guard the glen from penetrating ills,
Though torn the walls now, blank and blind,
They seem to know who passes in the hills.
Monuments of power, if for long decayed,
They keep their secrets, not afraid.

What men were here so long ago
Whose inward-looking monuments survive
The annual sacrifices to the skies
That hurl their wild bombardment –
Rain, winds, hail and snow –
Where no mysterious generations live
Of warriors lost? No battle-cries
Now echo in the glens. A few wild sheep,
Buzzards skimming hillcrests, humble juniper keep
The watch now on the winding glen below.

(1967)

By W E Yuill

THE ROMAN FOUNTAIN
(Der Römische Brunnen by C F Meyer)

Aufsteigt der Strahl und fallend giesst
Er zoll der Marmorschale Rund,
Die, sich verschleirnd, überfliesst
In einer zweiten Schale Grund;
Die zweite gibt, sie wird zu reich,
Der dritten wallend ihre Flut,
Und jede nimmt und gibt zugleich
 Und strömt und ruht.

Up soars the jet and falling fills
The marble basin's curving rim
That, veiled in water, overspills
To reach a second basin's brim;
The second sheds its lapping swell
To flood the third one as it goes,
And each one takes and gives as well,
 And rests and flows.

(1962)